Rosemary McGuire is from and of the cold latitudes about which she writes. It shows in the chop and bang, the beauty and slide of her words as if lifted directly from the Arctic's intrinsic difficulty and elegance. She is that rare Arctic worker, a jack of all trades: assistant to scientists, first mate, fisherman, solo river rat, as well as an historian and ethnographer, who has the ability to translate her varied experiences into this most astonishing memoir. Not to be missed!

—GRETEL EHRLICH, author of *Unsolaced*

Rosemary McGuire proves equally capable on the page and at sea. With language as striking as the unique landscapes she visits, she balances intrepid adventure with quiet introspection, wanderlust with reverence. From solo kayak expeditions to ice-encrusted commercial fishing vessels, *Cold Latitudes* carries readers to the fierce and fragile edges of the earth, always in good company.

—CAROLINE VAN HEMERT, author of *The Sun is Compass*

Rosemary McGuire has forged a remarkable life from traveling and working in the extremes of the Arctic and Antarctic. From her vantage as a lone kayaker, boat handler, fish tender, crew member, and technician on various scientific expeditions and projects, she interweaves her direct, open-hearted experience with critical aspects of history and science. The rapid change occurring in the high latitudes, both in the environment and in our scientific and Indigenous cultures, is clearly brought home in McGuire's precise and lyrical prose, which leaves a stunning afterglow to all she evokes.

—NANCY LORD, former Alaska writer laureate, author of *Beluga Days*, *Early Warming*, and *pH: A Novel*

T0099506

Rosemary McGuire writes beautifully about wilderness, harrowingly about danger, inspiringly about hard work. She has come up with ways to reach places few people see. Something profound is calling her, and in these chapters she takes us along on her search for the source.

—TOM KIZZIA, author of the New York Times bestseller *Pilgrim's Wilderness*

Cold Latitudes

Cold Latitudes

◆

Rosemary McGuire

ALASKA
LITERARY
SERIES

University of Alaska Press Fairbanks

Text © 2021 University of Alaska Press

Published by
University of Alaska Press
P.O. Box 756240
Fairbanks, AK 99775-6240

Cover and interior design by UA Press.

Cover image: *Cold Islands* (detail) by Asia Freeman,
oil on canvas, 36'' x 36'', 2015.

Library of Congress Cataloging-in-Publication Data

Names: McGuire, Rosemary Desideria, author.
Title: Cold Latitudes / by Rosemary McGuire.
Description: Fairbanks, AK : University of Alaska Press, [2021]
Identifiers: LCCN 2020030590 (print) | LCCN 2020030591 (ebook) |
ISBN 9781602234376 (paperback) | ISBN 9781602234383 (ebook)
Subjects: LCSH: Polar regions—Environmental conditions. |
Landscapes—Polar regions. | Climatic changes—Polar regions. |
Animals—Polar regions.
Classification: LCC G590 .M237 2021 (print) | LCC G590 (ebook) |
DDC 910.911—dc23
LC record available at https://lccn.loc.gov/2020030590
LC ebook record available at https://lccn.loc.gov/2020030591

for Ned

Contents

◆

Acknowledgments

◆

I would like to thank the hunters, community members, scientists, and others who have shared their lives and knowledge with me. Although some names have been changed at request, all stories in this book are true. I would also like to thank Peggy Shumaker, Frank Soos, Nate Bauer, Jessica Cherry, and others who helped greatly in the editorial process. Lastly, I would like to thank the children of Schloesser Road: Autumn, Ava, Torlief, Halfdan, and Gunnar. You listened to these stories first when I came home from far away.

Kongakut River, Easter Island

◆

August 2008, July 2013

Landing in Kaktovik, Dad and I saw a polar bear tearing at the bones of a whale cast up last year, looking for scraps left on the ribs. As we gathered our belongings by the landing strip, a woman stopped me. She did not tell me her name. She was so quiet her eyes hardly met mine, but she tried to warn me.

"Don't camp on the barrier islands. Camp on land. There are more bears on the islands."

I listened, nodding. Later, I wondered if that advice saved our lives. It was late summer. Dad and I had flown into Kaktovik on the Beaufort Sea coast, to paddle east along the barrier islands to the mouth of the Kongakut and line our canoe upriver, crossing the Brooks Range to the Sheenjek River drainage. But that summer the sea ice had retreated so far the bears could not reach it. Those left on land were struggling to survive.

It was foggy when we paddled out of Kaktovik. The strange Arctic light robbed us of perspective. At times we could no longer tell direction; the world melted into depthless distance. We camped that night on coastal tundra. As we sat outside our tent, we saw two polar bears moving toward us along the island nearest our camp. A mother and a yearling cub searching the bare sand for food. The channel between us was narrow, but they did not notice us.

The mother sank down on the sand to rest. Her cub splashed into the lagoon, swimming back and forth. It moved almost like a seal, its pelvis limber and wide, broad feet driving it forward.

At length, it left the water to rejoin its mother. We watched as they lay down together to sleep.

"Look," Dad said, quietly. We saw a grizzly coming from the opposite direction. Like them, it swung its head along the tideline, questing for food. As it came near, the wind carried its smell to the mother. She scrambled to her feet, facing the grizzly. It rose on its hind legs to look at her. For a moment, they stared each other down. Then the grizzly dropped to its feet with an audible "whuff," swung around, and went back the way it came. The mother and cub turned away, all three bears once more searching barren ground.

Slowly, I set the shotgun down. I'd felt some balance change between predator and prey. Here we were all the vulnerable ones.

The following day, we paddled outside the islands, past black bluffs softened by melting permafrost and torn by a roughening sea. It was cold; again the fog pressed against the water. That night we stopped on high ground marked with a weathered cross. It bore the names of a man and two young girls who died here while traveling between Kaktovik and Aklavik,

Kenneth Robert Peeloolok Paul b. 4/29/63
Sandra Denise Dolly Meyook b. 6/18/87
Sylvia Rose Lucy Meyook b. 2/21/83

They had drowned on August 23, 1999, when their skiff overturned in heavy seas. One of the girl's bodies was never found. It was a lonely thing to see, in a lonely place.

We camped there, partly for a strange kind of companionship. A ground squirrel peeked out to look at us, first from one hole, then another. At length it decided we were not a threat and went about its business, gathering seeds. Of all of us, it alone was making a home.

Next morning, the surf had built. We launched through it, all but swamping, and paddled down the outer coast, outside the sheltering barrier islands now, through a steel-gray, monotonous sea. The land a flat line under heavy cloud.

Late in the day, we saw another polar bear. We were offshore, paddling in a swell, already worrying about the wind, when we saw it. It seemed to apparate out of the sea; one moment not there, the next a solid white presence assessing our canoe. There was nothing we could do except to keep paddling; nowhere to go, and nowhere to hide.

Nose held high and easily pacing our canoe, it tracked us along the shore. I watched the grace of its gait, how it effortlessly moved over broken earth and ice. It seemed to have eight legs instead of four.

At last it turned and scrambled up a bluff of dark earth eroded by melting ice. We kept on as long as we could before we camped; knowing even so there was no way to leave its territory. We were in its place and on its terms.

Midmorning the following day, we reached the mouth of the Kongakut River. It fanned out in rivulets at the coast, choked with aufeis from the winter cold. Inland, it deepened abruptly into flood, churning green through gravel banks.

We rigged lines to our canoe and hauled it heavily upriver. Geese tracks and more bear sign marked the banks. Caribou and wolves, musk ox in scrub willow by the river.

On the third day, we reached the place where the Brooks Range rose abruptly from the coastal plain. The fog tore back. Mountains rose into blue sky over the clear, bright river, where fish hung in the pools as if suspended in air. Our spirits rose, too, with the light.

Three weeks in, we reached the mountain pass. It had frosted in the night, and the tundra was golden with fall, starred with dissolving ice as the sun hazed the sky east of us. In the morning we moved slowly, creakily, our bodies rejecting cold. I lit the fire while Dad gathered firewood.

He came back to tell me he'd seen a caribou near camp. "It has the most beautiful antler rack I've ever seen," he said.

I crunched after him over frozen grass. The caribou stood broadside to the sun near the river, unwilling to move even when it saw us. It was alone. South of us, the main herd would be passing, spilling through the Porcupine drainage to winter ground.

"The older bulls will do that," Dad said. "They'll go off by themselves. Quit migrating almost, before they die. This one won't last another winter."

As the light struck it, I could see a faint shimmer of vapor as the cold shifted from its back. On its head rose that astonishing rack. It was a perfect thing, but so heavy it seemed to bow the animal's head.

After a time, I went back to the fire. Dad stood for a long while watching, until the sun burned off the wonder of the morning. I thought he looked sad, but he never said what he was thinking.

The Sheenjek flowed into the Porcupine, the Porcupine into the Yukon River. Through the next days, falling down current, we passed through scrub willow golden with fall, into northern forest. Skeins of songbirds gathered, tying bright threads of flight across the sky. They linked a path through the faraway places of the world, joining them in one great highway.

The nights were cold. Wet socks and boots froze overnight. Mornings, we heard the call of swans and heard their heavy wings migrating south. I saw a wild rose, the last of summer, stiff with frost before dawn.

In late September we reached Fort Yukon. We pulled our canoe up the bank below the village and walked through half-deserted streets looking for the store. It was a lonely place so early in the day.

Tomorrow we would fly back to Fairbanks. Tired though we were, we felt half reluctant to go. We sat not talking much, eating ice cream on the steps of the village store. Thinking about the river. Thinking of what we lost as humankind when we lost our bond with such places. Lost some natural spirit.

Years have passed since that journey in the Brooks Range. The caribou must be long gone. My dad is older. I am too. Cold weather, the bedrock of our world, has become a thing that cannot be depended on, and development threatens the wilderness we journeyed. And yet, for now, the rivers still flow north and south, from a high, quiet place under an Arctic sky.

Long after that journey, I stopped once at Easter Island, traveling home from a job in the Southern Ocean. I was tired out from months of ice and snow and grueling work. I, too, tumbled from the sky as the birds do and washed up on a far-off shore, wanting nothing more than to watch the water, day after day, and feel the wind.

Easter Island, Rapa Nui, is a tiny, lonely island. Adrift in the blue waste of the Pacific, it hangs between two infinites, the unplumbable sky and the unknowable sea. Its shores are scraped bare of trees, long ago, by the first humans to arrive here. They were most likely Polynesian, a seafaring culture, skilled in ways we no longer understand at navigation and reading the sea. They arrived from somewhere far to the west, flourished here for a while, and passed away. It is said they may have died when they overran their resource base, cutting down the trees that made their canoes, unable then to use the sea. But their moas, stone statues, still remain as one of the great enigmas of the world. Their faces are closed and watchful, their makers gone.

The people died hard, they say. At the end, with nowhere to escape to, their world caved in to violence. Tribes killed tribes; families killed families. Rituals grew into rites of death and conquest. I saw caves in the rock where people hid to keep the other islanders from butchering them. The entrances rose dizzyingly high over the sea, it must have been an act of desperation just to reach those caves each day.

It is so quiet now on that island where the trade winds still blow and the surf breaks and breaks on the outer rocks. The moas brood over the shore, facing the sea. Little clear ripples roll in and vanish. But the people that came out of the sea long ago do not return and never will again.

And yet, a feeling hung over the island in the air, an abiding peace, a kind of deep remembering. There was a sadness to it, but a beauty too. Polynesians have a word, *mana*, for the "spirit that breathes out of places." It was there. For days I breathed it in, a lasting grace.

Leaving the river at Fort Yukon, we turned for one last look backward into time, at the river that rolled on to the sea without us now. I could not then and cannot now imagine the planet without wilderness. Something irreplaceable would vanish from our time. And so this is a love story for a threatened world.

Rivers, Solitaire

◆

June–July 2016

Under the bridge at Johnson's Crossing, swallows danced over the Teslin River. It was June, the water high with rain, the woods ragged with wild roses. I pushed my canoe out into the current, paddle strokes melting in my wake. Ice lay buried in the mud of the banks, and in places the water was up into the willows. Stalks of spring fireweed stood damp and green, half grown along the bank.

Wind stirred the river surface, the sun briefly golden. The last of the road, the last of houses and people slid behind me, and blue horizons stretched, leading north. There were no straight lines or depthless colors on the river. There was only me, my canoe, and the current; a feeling of quietness as I settled in to what was and had always been.

The Teslin drops into the Yukon; the Yukon flows to the Arctic Circle before bending west and south. It is a river too mighty to be ignored, a river with the gravitas of a sea. All my life, I'd wanted to follow it. All my life, I'd let it pass. But now I'd returned to it, this river, draining the taiga watershed where I was born, the center of Alaska.

Now my world was here in this small canoe, bent with hard use, its aluminum worked with age until it seemed almost pliable, and a slow leak coming through the floor. My dad and I had resurrected it as best we could the night before I headed to the river. It had traveled the Yukon many times before I was born, in company with a trapper, Charlie Wolf. I, too, knew my way, perhaps as well as most. But what I had not expected was to be so ambushed by memory and by the loneliness I tried to hold at bay. The river gives you so much time to remember as you pass from bend to bend, tracing progress on a blue line on a folded map, damp-smeared and crumpled in its sleeve. The river moves so slowly beside your own mind, until at last it is your mind.

When I stopped at my parents' house for this canoe, it had been years since I had gone home. There were always reasons, but one of them was that it reminded me so of how much things had changed; how much I, too, had changed over the years, through a sad marriage and subsequent hard divorce; the mire of minor struggles that can make a life.

The river crept slowly between the hills. At first my eyes rejected it for what it was. And then at last I saw what was really there. Near nightfall I passed a mother moose standing on the riverbank. She held so still, I thought at first she was a shadow, until I saw the marigold brightness of her calf, so new it was almost wet. I saw her umbilicus hanging. Her calf tried to stand and fell, tried and fell, its legs an impossibly ungainly bundle of stalks. Her eyes tracked me as I passed.

Two loons paralleled me for a time, their calls harsh with surprise each time they surfaced. A young beaver swam below the bank watching me, until the silence shattered with a slap of its tail on water in belated alarm. Behind him, the northern taiga stretched to

Siberia in an impassable tangle of wild roses and fallen logs, disorienting, seemingly endless. Still early in the season, it looked so green. The birds were making nests, bears stretching out of hibernation. At dusk, I heard wolves call, a hollow sound at the edge of hearing.

Three days in, silty fingers of the Yukon churned into the flooded Teslin. The current picked up speed, carrying me toward Dawson. Years ago, this was a highway to the north. Han Athapascan people used it as a trade route. They were followed by the voyageurs, by Hudson Bay trappers and gold seekers, by hunters, and by homesteaders going north.

Early next morning, I reached Five Finger Rapids. People drowned here in gold rush times, their makeshift crafts crushed against the rocks. But I was lucky; when I passed, the rapids were no more than a long stretch of swift water. Granitic columns rose in the river center, breaking it into five channels. Standing waves rose at the foot, but the water level drowned the riffles. I took the right-hand channel, as I'd been told, and shot through, balancing in the current, then pushed on, moving fast in sun and wind.

Nearing the White River, an old burn reached the river's edge. Black, charred trunks of dead spruce rose from a puff of fireweed stalks. The woods were silent, dense with summer heat. Gravel bars shone bright with a million stones; the surface of the water like mercury. Ahead, a duckling bobbed and skittered against the riverbank, peeping frantically for its lost mother. I swept past, and as I did I saw swift movement on the far bank. A black wolf bounded out of the willows; its ears pricked toward the sound. It shot a glance at me, looked at the duckling, and trotted upstream after it, tail arched, in fluid motion. They passed out of sight above the willows, the duckling still crying, the wolf, curious, prancing after it.

I passed White River, milky with glacial silt, its current so fast that even here it carried rock from the coastal range. On the mountainside above the water, I saw a grizzly rooting in the burned earth for shreds of new grass. A line of volcanic ash scarred the banks in chalk-pale drifts from an eruption more than a thousand years ago. Here and there, the river cut sharply through basalt, old lava flows that cooled on the surface of the land.

Alaska formed when the Brooks Range swung into place, during the Cretaceous period. Slowly, as tectonic plates pushed north, more land accreted against those early mountains and buckled upward into successive mountain ranges. The White Mountains, the Alaska Range, the Wrangells, each younger than the others. The Yukon itself formed after the Brooks Range. It was diverted by those pre-existing mountains, even as other mountains rose along its watershed. Meanwhile, the tectonic activity that formed those ranges also caused volcanic eruptions, as the earth's crust crumpled over millions of years.

I was traveling now into Beringia, an area that had been grassland steppe during the Pleistocene. Bordered by the Mackenzie River in Canada on the east and the Lena River in Siberia on the west, Beringia was unglaciated in the last Ice Age, its snowfall too light to form ice. It had encompassed the Bering Land Bridge, where once people walked across from Asia. In those days, so much seawater was locked in ice that the floors of many shallow seas were exposed. People had crossed, in successive bands. The genes of those first travelers spread through the New World, as they walked south through the continent.

Early evening in late June, I reached Dawson. Rainy, windy, cold, crowded with tourists in bright polyester outfits, and with kitschy gold rush paraphernalia, it seemed like a town constantly reinventing itself. I heard the rattle of a piano playing in a bar. Inside, the evening was a kaleidoscope of color and noise. When I stood to go, a little drunk, the room tilted around me. I passed a table of older folks by the door, their faces lit with happiness at being there together, despite the summer rain. They smiled at me, and I at them.

Founded by miners on the site of a Han Athapascan hunting camp, Dawson rose out of raw ground in the fall of 1897. That spring, three men—Tagish Charley, George Carmack, and Skookum Jim—had found gold on Bonanza Creek, in the Klondike. The news went out over the telegraph wires to an America hungry for excitement. Over the summer, men poured north into the territory, unprepared for the winter to come, and were caught by freeze-up here at Dawson. Hungry, cold, and without adequate shelter, they crowded streets deep with frozen mud.

That first winter was the hardest one. Two years later, Dawson had forty thousand people, dance halls, banks, and gambling saloons. Then, in 1899, the gold rush ended. All but a few of the prospectors vanished, leaving Dawson almost a ghost town. Until now, when hopeful tourists bring fresh cash in search of gilded memories.

Out in the street again, I stopped to see the pictures in a small, deserted museum. Photographs of miners and tightly corseted women lined the walls, a timeline of the boom and bust. The story of a mother who'd come north to find her son after his letters stopped arriving back home. She stayed in the Yukon Territory for the rest of her life but never found him. It was easy for me to imagine how he might have vanished. A capsized raft. A path lost somewhere in the woods. Easy for him never to be found.

Next morning, the rain had stopped. I headed back to the river in a gleam of watery sunshine, happy to be moving once again.

Below the Fortymile River, I passed the site of a boom that once had rivaled Dawson's. Now, the townsite stood deserted in a patch of fireweed and dense grass where the clear Fortymile River tumbled into the silt-green Yukon. I got out there, looking at log buildings built a hundred years before. It was so quiet, wild roses the only inhabitants.

Years ago, my parents lived on mining land in Interior Alaska, on Happy Road near Fairbanks. They built a cabin there and raised four children before moving to Haines, in Southeast Alaska. Happy Road in those days had many homesteads on mine claims, small places with small children and husky dogs. It was a place of bright-leaved birch trees, bluebells, and heavy mud in early spring. No one could drive it during breakup, when the land melted and snow ran off. The mud lay deep, drying from the top down; a child could bounce on its hard surface, over the still-liquid depths, and feel the road move under foot. My sister and I played in the mud, coming home dirty, chilled, and tired in the thin, bright sunlight of May afternoons, to where my mother dunked us in the rain barrel. We had imaginary horses, fairy houses, a playhouse under the trees. In spring, when the yard flooded, we waded from birch to birch in water as cold as snow. It was a place where everybody seemed so young.

Then one spring, we left Happy Road. All the families did, at the same time. Alaska was changing. The pipeline had come the year that I was born on Happy Road, and the federal government was reorganizing land rights. You could no longer live forever on a mining claim.

We moved down to the coast in Southeast Alaska and lived for a time in a tent while Dad built another cabin on the shore. I loved the ocean too. My sister and I learned to paddle a canoe and spent long afternoons reading Nancy Drew mysteries in the front seat of the pickup while the rain kept falling. But I was older then. The world looked different. It was more coherent, less full of wonder and imminent, golden color. But I remembered spring days in the mud, and where we came from, in the north.

Now I pushed off and headed down the Yukon again. The river grew wind-ripped, a thing of shifting bars and wicked current. Next morning, I woke to the sound of a swan calling for its mate. No one answered. It called again and flew through my camp with heavy wingbeats. As light hit the tent, I unzipped the fly, and saw smoke veiling the sun, and a gray fall of ash on the canvas. On each side, the river parted into riffles, enclosing the gravel bar where I'd camped late last night. Far downriver, the swan kept calling, vanishing.

By late morning, the sky grew fully dark as the smoke thickened from a forest fire somewhere. Landmarks were erased by blowing smoke. I could no longer see the riverbanks. I hoped I was not paddling into the fire, but I had little choice. The river went where it wanted to, and I went too.

In summertime, on Happy Road, the summer forest fires began. They, too, were a part of the northern taiga. I remember standing in the yard with my family, looking up at the red coin of the sun and seeing wild geese, confused by the smoke, sweep through the yard, flying lower than the treetops. They veered in surprise when they saw us. My mother's goats blatted in alarm at the smell of burning, and the dogs barked uneasily at no one. We children moved closer to our parents. The smoke grew denser until we could hardly breathe, but the fire moved west and we never had to leave.

Each season, old burns were replaced with new growth. Fireweed and grass, morel mushrooms and wild blueberries grew over blackened earth. Then came alder, birch, and spruce; deep tundra on the swampy bitter soil over permafrost. Rosehips and wild cranberries, viburnum, bear bread, Labrador tea. I picked the cranberries with my sister, and my mother stored them in the cold cellar for winter; she made tea of the rosehips, preserved the blueberries.

In winter, in those days, cold was something that lay on the land, pooling in the lowest places. Skiing downhill, you could feel it strike your face with palpable weight when you reached the river bottoms. Sounds magnified in the dense air; twigs broke frighteningly loud. Breath burned in the lungs, and cold needled in through the smallest gaps in clothing. Nothing moved but the ravens.

In still, deep cold, you could stand outside and look at the stars pricking through a blanket of night during the shortest days of the year. When the sun rose, it rolled along the horizon, never quite leaving the lowest part of the sky, as if it, too, had grown heavy with the cold. Light turned turquoise and red and gold; the snow-scrubbed wilderness seemed to burn with a cold fire.

On a night like that, lasting until noon, we kids loaded into the pickup and were taken to town to see Blue Babe. Found in a placer mine near Fairbanks, Blue Babe was a bison that had been killed by an American lion thirty-six thousand years before. A friend of my parents had prepared it for the university museum. We kids stood outside the smeared glass case peering in. The bison knelt, head low as if accepting its fate, muzzle almost touching the ground. Its horns looked heavy. The hide on its back was scored with the long claw marks of the lion. You could see the thickness of the hide, and the wrinkles in it at the animal's joints. It was all still perfect and still there. The skull of a lion, its front fangs bared, hung in a different case. It was easy to see how this had happened. These were creatures from the recent past that still haunted our memories and dreams. And yet how much the world had changed.

On shore, the forest fires growing fiercer now, the summers hotter, and the land perhaps returning to grasslands. As it had been in the Pleistocene when Blue Babe died. As it had been when these layers of silt laid down, crosscut in the riverbanks, as the river kept on laying down and refilling, turning over the layers of the past, rebuilding them, remaking the land.

The fire now burned sullenly, the canoe outpaced it. The sun faded as the sky grew dim, in an indistinguishable smear of light. The smoke clung in my throat and eyes, tiring me. It was hard to breathe, and the wind kept rising in my face. Nothing moved on the river but myself.

Late evening, well past the fire, exhausted, I stopped to camp at the water's edge, feeling the renewed clench of isolation after the trial of the day. The aching, acrid smell of smoke dying on the wind.

"I wish I had someone to talk to," I said aloud. At that moment, I heard small footsteps in the grass. A porcupine shuffled slowly, steadily toward me.

Magically, I thought, "Could it have heard?"

I held still as it came closer, its barbed tail rustling the earth. A small animal, defenseless against fire. It had lived long, though, in its way, wild in forests unburned as yet. And it could hurt me, I was still in its place.

"You're frightening me," I said at last, softly.

It halted in its tracks. Turned nearsighted eyes to look at me first from one side, then the other. Set a foot down slowly and returned the way it came. A moment later I heard it again. It circled behind me to climb the spruce I sat beneath, at the edge of the slough. I wondered why that tree mattered so much to it, that it would risk my presence to reach it. We were each afraid of each other, and yet somehow, its nearness comforted me. We were companions in our solitude, our vulnerability, living things with private enterprises, each seeking food and shelter in our way. Too, it was so perfectly what it was, so much a part of this forest; if it were gone, a still small voice would leave this wilderness.

Two nights later, above Circle, the smoke cleared. The following afternoon, the wind switched north and grew stronger. I was forced ashore onto a gravel bar. As I pulled in, I saw more smoke ahead at the mouth of the Tatondek River. It eddied from a bluff of pinkish rock. As night came on, I watched it rise and fall, rise and fall.

I'd landed on a drying silt bar scarred by winter ice and high-water currents. Just before dark, I walked it looking for animal tracks. I saw none. It was a lonely feeling, those washes of unpatterned sand, where before the shores had been traced with many tracks.

Through hundreds of river miles to come in Alaska, it was the same. I saw no wolves on the Alaska Yukon and few bears. I did not understand it at the time. I just kept traveling. But later, back in town, I learned about the state's wolf control program, and how they'd shot packs near that stretch of river. I wondered if that had been the cause. It was hard to know, and harder still to understand the reasoning. The justification was to artificially enhance popula-tions of game animals. But moose are often limited not by predation but by habitat and by availability of browse. And meanwhile, the land had fallen silent.

Sleeping alone in a tent in the wilderness is an act of trust that may not always be justified. I am not a brave woman. I knew there was a real possibility a wild animal could hurt me. But I wouldn't choose to have them hunted out for my convenience, or to see as I did then, my own tracks as the only tracks on a month's worth of drying river silt. To be the only species living is a kind of death.

I stayed with the river until it crossed the Arctic Circle then left it for a while to work. Two of my uncles drove me to Fairbanks over Eagle Summit, under a summer moon, to my sister's cabin on a dirt road near where we grew up. Fireweed bloomed in the yard of the cabin, untrampled by feet since I left. The rain had found a new pathway through the roof. I spread my tent to dry on the porch, unpacked my food, made a fire in the stove. Even the fire seemed different there from on the river, both more protected and somehow less true.

Near the end of summer, I returned to the Yukon along the Chandalar, which flows south from the Brooks Range. In August I reached the edge of the Yukon Flats again. That morning, it began to rain as I broke camp, a steady, soaking drizzle that ceased as I paddled on to Venetie. The river seemed low, a trickle of water switchbacking between scrub willows.

Fireweed had bloomed out along the shore, in hollows where the earth was torn, and now the puffs of seeds had faded too. Ten years ago on the Colleen River, my dad and I climbed a bank into a little hollow full of fireweed stalks drying in the sun. As I stood there, suddenly the breeze caught them and the puffs of their white seeds swirled up and away all around me, gone almost before I could say I had seen them, gone so quickly with the summer and sunlight of that day.

I tied my canoe up by a line of river boats lying on the bank and pushed through alder on a trail lined with broken-down heavy equipment, up to buildings lost in the rain. Three men sat drinking coffee on the porch of the general store. They asked where I was bound. When I told them, they joked, "Take me with you."

There was a kind of wistfulness and wanting behind the joke. One told me how he'd once made ratting canoes out of canvas stretched over a pole frame, in the old days, the old days on the river.

"Small but good canoes," he said. "It's been a long time since I went in a canoe."

"The river's changing," he added. "It's changing fast. You don't see beaver like you used to, or bears."

He tapped out his cigarette. The rain began to fall again. In the whole village, nothing else seemed to move. There was a kind of permanent stillness in the air and a sadness in the men on the porch.

"You going on today?" he asked.

I told him yes, and he said. "If you ever have nowhere to go, you can come back to Venetie. We'll be here."

I hoped it was true.

He walked with me for company as I went back to the river, through the fireweed and the rain, to my canoe. I half expected it, too, would have slipped away like a half-used dream.

Herring, Norton Sound

◆

April–June 2006
Winters 2010–2011

It was blowing when we left Cordova, heading west for spring herring. Slush smeared the wheelhouse windows. Inside, the red lights gave a temporary illusion of warmth. But it was so cold, the wind crept through the dogged-down wheelhouse doors. And the *Jamie D* rocked heavily, too high and flat-bottomed for such weather.

The *Jamie D* had been built as an oil research vessel in the Amazon River basin and had come here to Alaska, at the end of its life, almost by accident. Its decks shone marigold, sharp with flaking rust, and deep in the engine room, pools of cold oil formed under the engines that coughed a steady drone, thrusting us west. No telling how many miles under its keel, or how much done well or badly in its wake. Men had died on here; others had made money, and faraway, there were many shores it had worked along, sometimes doing harm, perhaps sometimes good.

Now we were headed west, across the Sound, past the Kenai Peninsula, through the ship's boneyard of Shelikof Strait, and through False Pass into the Bering Sea. It was April, herring season in Alaska. We had a contract to tender, buying herring from the fishermen out west and transporting it to catcher processors. In the wheelhouse, one of the men stood slowly, repetitively kicking the wheel to starboard. The autopilot was so old no one could program it; it was set for the magnetic declination of the equator. So we steered rhythmically to starboard, to offset its drift. Night was coming down; the weather closing in early. We'd hoped to chase a weather window, but it closed as we were leaving the dock. We left anyway, afraid to stay, afraid of losing crew to the bars or to second thoughts. Four of us on here: myself, the skipper, a deckhand from Florida, and Tony, a silent man, not yet a friend but already an ally.

Salmo Point, Simpson Bay, Sheep Bay, and Gravina. Familiar landmarks fell behind. As we neared Knowles Head, the seas began to build, the wheelhouse dipping now in a long perpetual swing, side to side like a pendulum, that would become more and more familiar in months to come. Years back there'd been a herring fishery in these waters too. But Prince William Sound herring died when the *Exxon Valdez* tanker spilled oil into these waters in 1989, and they had not recovered, for reasons not yet wholly understood. Herring is a keystone species that drives vitality through whole ecosystems, but they are very vulnerable to contaminated waters. The repercussions from their loss were felt through the chain of life and nowhere more than now in spring, when the burst of life—birds, fish, whales—that blooms along the Alaska coast when herring spawn did not come here.

We anchored that night behind Amatuli Island, letting the weather blow past for a time. The boat was cold, damp, with a strange, unforgettable smell, composed, I thought, of long nights and loneliness.

Past Shelikof Strait, we ran down the Alaska Peninsula. Past Pavlov Bay, the wind shrieked down the bay with miles of fetch, pinning us suddenly. The anemometer pegged at sixty. Shores streaked with winter snow, the sky hard gray, seas racing under our rail. Heavy thunk-thunk of engines. We stood watch two at a time now. Every half hour someone checked the engine room. We were afraid of what might happen if we did not. No alarms were working. Meanwhile, the other watch-stander clung to the wheel, steadily turning, starboard, starboard, starboard, a motion that seemed to creep into our souls.

We turned west again through False Pass, at the tip of the Alaska Peninsula. Too shallow there for the largest ships to go through, so shallow that the seas built high. We picked our way from buoy to buoy. But the buoys seemed to have been dragged off station by winter ice. We could hear a Coast Guard ship nearby, talking of resetting them. Ahead, a crabber headed through. We followed them, knowing from their voices over the radio that they were drunk, and also that they still might know more about the pass than we did. These seas were too dynamic to trust the charts; there was only local knowledge to be relied on year by year, and the Coast Guard buoys when they were in place.

I said something in a low voice.

"Shut up, Rose," the skipper said, and so I knew he was afraid too.

Tony stood by me, his face impassive, a wad of snooze in his lip, spitting in a cup. His first child, a son, was born two days before we left Cordova. He took this job to pay the bills.

"Rose?" he said now, almost too quietly to hear. "Did you check the survival suits before we left?"

"Yeah," I said.

"I can't swim," he said.

I nodded. "I did it. For sure."

"Thanks," he said. From then on, we were friends.

Through False Pass the seas grew more regular as the water deepened. We turned north again, heading for Nunivak, past Bristol Bay, which in summer held the largest red salmon run in the world. Past Cape Constantine, a weather breeder. The shores were no longer mountainous; instead we passed low tundra hills, seemingly stripped of human presence, though they had been inhabited for thousands of years. These people chose to leave no trace on these wild shores.

Past Round Island, where walrus gathered in spring. Two of them swam out deep, near the boat. They dove when they saw us, disappearing in a splash of silty gray water. Past the Nushagat River.

On the third night, we pulled into Togiak, dropped the anchor, and fell asleep. When I woke, I saw there was no harbor and no town in sight. We lay in the lee of a long peninsula, on the edge of the herring fishing grounds. When the fishery began we would buy herring from the fishing boats and ferry it to the processor. But there was no shore base to the fisheries there. The local people launched in spring from small boats dragged up on land on rollers, but the flat, silty shore did not allow for natural harbors, and most of the fleet came from far away.

Other boats had anchored there already, hiding from the weather. Pack ice still lay along the shore. Low sand dunes shaped by wind. Tundra golden with winter grass in the first light. Silver water in the leads. Not a sound but wind and birds. The sun came up, a soft flame hanging like the moon. It was beautiful.

But we were early for the season. The herring were "green," the Alaska Department of Fish and Game biologist told us over the VHF radio, not yet near spawning. Herring spawn all at once when the water temperature hits a certain window. That spawn drives an explosion of life. Gray whales migrate thousands of miles for it, birds as well. Now we hunkered down to wait, whales surfacing around us, ducks splattering the storm-torn water. Everything was waiting. Everything was waiting to live.

Once, in early spring, I worked on a research boat in Prince William Sound, studying the loss of herring there. A blue steel boat, deep draft, overcrowded with scientists and techs. I was the deck-hand for the crew. At night we did acoustic surveys, mapping density of young herring that surfaced in the dark, and cast netting for fry. In the early hours before dawn, we started hauling longlines set for predator fish to see what was eating the juvenile herring. Slowly, those cold mornings began, ice on the decks, the sunlight coming up until it made the water smoke. Dawn brought a chorus of birds, high whistles from murrelets seeking the forest. Then as gray light faded into blue, ravens stirred, a few ducks lifted from the water, their wings blurring a whistle sound.

Sometimes the decks were deep in snow. Or we woke to the crystal purity of winter blue skies. The water was so clear in wintertime, though it would green and blur when the spring came and phytoplankton bloomed. We heard falling water everywhere; the frozen rivers hanging overhead were still traced with currents too quick to staunch entirely.

But the herring were not there, as they should have been. Juvenile herring overwinter in Prince William Sound and begin migrating after their first year of life. We found many fry but few first-year fish. Somehow they were not surviving their first winter of life. Yet the predator fish we caught contained few herring. They were not being eaten by the resident species of the Sound.

Nighttimes around the galley table, as we sat in darkness doing lightless acoustic surveys, the crew talked of what we saw. Again and again I heard the thought floated that this might be the work of salmon hatcheries. In the years after the oil spill, many hatcheries were built in Prince William Sound, churning out sockeye, pink, and dog salmon fry. The fry were raised from fish eggs collected in the summer, released in the spring to out-migrate, and caught by commercial fishermen when they returned a year or two or many later. The hatcheries had saved the commercial industry around Cordova, some thought. Others questioned that. But it was a hard question to raise in public, in a fishing town, so isolated, so close-knit and dependent on the fish that were our treasure.

But were hatchery fish exceeding the carrying capacity of the Sound? How long could it last? The fry could be eating the juvenile herring when in their floods of millions they were released from the hatcheries each spring; or they could be simply outcompeting them for food. No one knew. It was easier to blame the oil spill. But for all the demonstrable and irremediable harm done by the spill to the Sound, it was possible that the loss of herring was not merely the result of actions done by some "other." It might have been our work as well, our work as fishermen.

It was no secret that the hatchery fish were straying, breeding in wild streams and weakening the genetic stock of the wild salmon. It was no secret wild salmon were growing smaller, as if the ocean could not feed so many fish. No secret that the Sound had changed; only a stranger could see this as a place untouched, wild as it looked. And yet how to tease out from this tangle of causes, one root cause, if there even was one? Studies were funded, cancelled, or extended as a way, it seemed, of not confronting the problem, but only, always, researching further, as if we were all afraid what we might find. But meanwhile the sun rose over the beautiful islands. And still, there was so much richness in the world.

The day after we arrived at Togiak, the floating processors came, huge structures like factories on water. The *Bering* and the *Aleutian Falcon*. When we went alongside, the faces of the deckhands peered down. None looked happy. It was lunchtime, and the boat smelled of old grease from the cafeteria, souring the blue, sunny day.

The skipper backed up and pulled forward several times, trying to get us in tight to the *Falcon's* side. We struck them hard. The steel rebounded, and the boats sprang apart. Deckhands ran along the *Falcon's* deck, shrieking in Spanish. One man hurled me a line. I pulled it in hand over hand until the heavy hawser came, while the *Jamie D* ground against their side.

The skipper came out of the wheelhouse once we tied up. He lit a cigarette with hands that shook.

"I hate fucking current," he said. "I had it in mind that if I wrecked this boat I'd never go back to Cordova again." He flipped his smoke unfinished over the rail. "Guess I'll go apologize."

He climbed onto the *Falcon* and disappeared. I sat on the fish pump, making a throwing stone out of scrap steel and a hank of twine.

In half an hour the skipper came back for me. "Manager wants to teach you how to make fish tickets," he said. "How to report the poundage each boat delivers, that kind of thing."

I swung over the rail and followed him, up one ladder and another, along narrow, dirty halls until we came to a great, cluttered, overwarm wheelhouse stuffed with cell phones and radios, stacks of paperwork, and big-bellied American men. The manager showed me a complicated system of forms, papers for the deck boss, papers for the skipper, for us, for the fishermen, and for Fish and Game. A log to keep track in, and how to calculate percentages of herring roe, pounds on board, and temperatures.

As we were leaving, he offered me a stack of magazines, back issues of *Cosmopolitan* and *Vogue* left by the cook, an enormous man. I did not want them, but the skipper picked them up.

"The guys will like 'em," he said. "They've got pictures."

"Of sulky people in strange hats?"

"Anything," he said. "Once boredom sets in it's a disease."

I followed him down the narrow halls. "Listen," he said, "there's gonna be a hell of a current when we leave here. I want you to get a buoy on the bow. I'll pivot on that, try and get the stern around and give us some clearance. Yeah?"

Back on the boat, I took a buoy from the rail and wedged it in along our bow. The skipper ground the bow hard into the side of the processor, trying to get our stern around, until the buoy lay knuckled flat and groaning under the weight of steel. He threw the boat in reverse then, and we shot back, but the current sucked us hard against the *Falcon*. We deckhands ran to the back deck to get out of the way. Our rigging dragged along their stern, just where it curved, dragged a little, almost lightly. Then we were under their stern and clear. I went back to the wheelhouse and saw the skipper still clutching the wheel.

"Fuck," he said. "We almost lost it that time."

Later, he sent me in to the village of Togiak to expedite supplies. I went on a helicopter from the processor. It seemed to fall away into space from the side of the boat. When we landed, the earth seemed to move under my feet. I thought I was swaying until I realized it was only because I'd been on a boat for so long.

Outside, the dirt roads of the village lay flooded with meltwater, their margins packed deep with rotting snow. Two old women passed on an ATV, riding slowly so as to not get wet. They waved at me. Boats stood on blocks along the waterfront. None looked rigged or ready to go herring fishing. A rubble of ice piled around them, gray and marred by snowmachine tracks and shell casings.

When my work was done, I waited by the deserted gravel airstrip for the chopper. Sleet began to fall. An older man waved from the porch of a cabin by the runway.

"Come on over. I'll make you hot chocolate," he said.

"It's my Christian duty," he explained when I came nearer.

I followed him in to the single room of his cabin and sat at the kitchen table while he made hot chocolate. He showed me a pine grosbeak he'd found dead on the shore, a bird from the inland forests gone astray. It was wrapped in plastic, in his freezer, along with several others I did not recognize.

"Accidentals, they call them," he said. "Blown here from Asia, or the Interior."

He spoke slow and quiet. I listened, quiet too. When I heard the chopper coming, I went back to the airstrip. It was blowing hard now, and the ride was difficult. I was glad to reach the boat again.

By early May, gray whales fished around the boat each morning, surfacing with soft breaths and going under. Black cormorants ran in Vs across the water. Their wings made an almost tinkling sound in the cold air. I climbed up on the chain locker in the morning and sat to watch the flat line of the coast and the wind-stirred water. Boats had anchored all around us now. But in the whole landscape, there was nothing of human scale. Only a troubling vastness of sea and sky. Here were men with no other interest in this place but a knowledge of the fish. And all of us were standing at the edge of something great we did not understand.

Overhead, a flock of scoters pattered by, almost too far away for me to see. They left here, and they always came back, but which was home to them? Or did they come only to leave again? Was their home only in this oscillation, this endless crossing of the sea in search of a destination that existed only in the imagination, receding even as they attained it?

I thought of it a moment, but my mind fell back. I couldn't conceive of a world so large. Instead, I wondered if someday when the tide of commerce no longer washed up on these bare shores, what would have changed. The rocks and ice would outlast us, though we killed the fish. It seemed to me as though the world might be the better for our vanishing.

After a while, Tony came out to sit with me. He lit a cigarette and smoked as we talked. He wore three sweatshirts layered together and a watch cap borrowed from the skipper.

"I didn't know what to pack for this," he said. "They said, 'Out west,' but I didn't know what it would be like. How do you figure all these birds find their way back up here?"

"I think they're born with mental compasses," I said.

"I wish I was," he said, looking lost. He tucked his hands in his pockets and drew his knees up on the chain locker.

The following morning, the skipper took me to land. Driving the skiff, he was smiling in the sunshine and the wind of our passing. I could smell the tundra as I stepped ashore, winter grasses dampening with rain and seeds opening. Beach grass and Queen Anne's lace, with its knobby roots and complicated leaves, sprouted under shrinking snow. Lichen covered the barest ground, deep berry red and golden, brilliant orange. I knelt to stare at them and smell the ground. It was so detailed and alive after so many weeks of sea and sky. My heart swelled sharply with a joy that was almost awe.

Walking west along the coast, I saw ground squirrel claws lying naked on the grass and vertebrae still darkened with new blood. Wolf scat full of seagull feathers. On shore, under a ledge of melting ice, I

saw sea lion bones, green and soft with age. Plover, feeding with con-
centrated force, scuttled at the water's edge. They moved as one bird,
drifting now together and apart, but all aiming—scuttle—stop—to
the same place.

Twisted in sea wrack, I found the body of one that had drowned.
I picked it up and turned it in my hands. It was so fine and light, its
black feet and its bill like needles. It seemed wrong that it should be
so dead. I wondered what had killed it. An offshore wind too strong
to overcome?

"Everything dies," I said aloud. "It's nothing to cry over."

I set it down, and walked away again. But that evening as I
waited for the skipper to come for me, I saw fishermen with guns
going ashore. They lined up on the coast to the east of us and shot
at flocks of shorebirds as they went over. I watched the birds tumble
broken to the ground and realized the men weren't even bothering to
pick up what they killed. It was target practice to them.

In mid-May, the work began at last. Fish and Game announced
an opener one night. The next morning we got up at five o'clock.
The skipper was on edge, wanting to take fish so we could see if
everything worked. I, too, felt lightheaded after a time. I sat up in
the wheelhouse, watching the boats cluster and disperse by shore,
the whole circus of seiners and tenders in slow motion. Fish spilled.
Sea lions circled, bursting out of the water and then gone. It was very
quiet. And it seemed as though this had always been happening and
always would be, us idling offshore away from the half-lazy, half-
violent turn of event.

In the afternoon, we were called in to the *Razor's Edge*. They had
wrapped up a big set, maybe two hundred tons of herring, and their
net was sinking. They needed help.

The skipper edged us through a crowd of other seiners. We tried to get hooks on the net to hold up the cork line, but there were so many fish we couldn't lift it. The herring quivered, circled by the net; the school swam tighter and tighter, black backs turning and diving, swirling into dizziness, and as they dived the net began to sink. We got the crane hook on to lift the cork line, but the *Jamie D* began drifting back. I struggled with the net and struggled to hear the skipper's voice over the crashing noise of wind and engines.

Once we got the seine hooked up, we lowered the submersible fish pump from the crane. It was meant to suck the fish out of the net through a series of pipes, over a superstructure on our back deck, and into the hold. But it failed to work. Instead, it chopped the herring into a bloody foam until the skipper slowed it almost to a crawl. Even after that, the herring did not slide into the hold. I climbed up on the pump and shoved them along, using my arms as sweepers. It was cold up there, and windy, but we couldn't stop. The herring piled up, slid forward in little jerks, and plunged into the hold. Hours passed, ton by ton.

"That's a goddamn slow pump," the skipper of the *Razor's Edge* said, fretfully.

The skipper got him a beer. They stood kicking their feet against the deck, making conversation. But it seemed as if each was talking in a void, taken up by thoughts they could not share. I stood on the pump and listened as I worked. Pinned my gaze to the swirling fish and to the chunks of brilliant roe that they expelled, the roe for which this whole show came to be. The herring had come so far, to end up like this.

Next morning, the wind was high, blowing from the north. There wasn't much sea-room for the waves to build, but the wind itself had a violent edge that seemed to promise more to come. I sat in the swaying wheelhouse with the skipper, watching the silver, glassy water whipped to froth and scudding clouds over snow-streaked mountains. Watching our ETA to the processor recede and recede as the seas picked up. Telling stories. A time he dragged a fisherman out of the breakers on the Copper River flats.

"We got a towline on him, God knows how. We were all fucked up. There was a company rep on board, observing the fishery, and he told us, 'That was a Coast Guard quality rescue,' but it wasn't . . . it was stupid luck. We should've all been dead that time."

Near Hagemeister, we passed another vessel. They had their net out and had blown down on it, trying to get it back. Their skiff was half-sinking. The skipper radioed to ask if they needed help.

"No, we got 'er," the skipper came back, growling.

That night, the *Razor's Edge* managed to make a set in the lee of the island. He called us, and we went to pick him up. It took three tries to get the seine tied up. The wind whipped hard, blowing us around. The skipper had his son in the skiff, towing. The kid looked worn out, but his father kept yelling.

"Hey, kid. Tow a little smarter."

There was nothing we could do to help. We pumped their seine and went away.

From Nunivak, when the season ebbed, we went north again up the long coast to Norton Sound. All day the mountains assumed ever more fantastic shapes, fractured and fountaining towers of rock. They loomed far off on a blue horizon. If the land was flat it would have sunk under the curve of the world. We were far out on the Bering Sea.

For most of the day we were ahead of the processor fleet, but pack ice turned us back in Etolin Strait. We had to wait for the rest of the fleet to catch up, to follow them north. They had a helicopter to guide them through leads in the ice.

It was a clear, warm evening. Calm and blue. Nothing to be seen but a little haze and the low white line of the pack ice to starboard. I sat talking in the wheelhouse with the skipper, the breeze coming in the open doors. It was tense for a while that day with the ice and even out of sight of land so shallow that once we thought we'd go aground. But even so, somehow I wished we could keep heading north until we reached the edge of the world.

Midmorning the following day, the convoy caught up to us. We fell in line behind them. Three tenders, the processors, and a Russian freighter, *Snow Mass*. We broke through ice where we'd turned back the day before, pushing loose floes out of the way. Whales spouted in the lead before us. I stood on the bow to watch, seeing the floes part and sink under the boat and emerge slowly, turning red with rust and bottom paint. Once we went up on a larger floe, and it swung us sideways, helpless, feeling the deep shock of ice on steel.

As the Russian *Snow Mass* came through, the skipper called the *Falcon* on the radio, asking for help.

"Please," he said. "Please, we would like to know our future."

"Me too," Tony said, deadpan.

Somehow, that struck us as funny. We were all a little mad with excitement in the pure, cold sunshine of the sea. We laughed, staring at the ice. It parted before us, and we were free, running through open water for Cape Vancouver.

"Fuck," the skipper said, smiling, "somebody get me a cigarette. For a while there, I thought we were going to end up as a headline."

"I already was a headline once," one of the other deckhands said. "'Rash of Burglaries Baffles Police.' I was so proud I clipped it out and showed my dad. But he turned me in."

"Your dad turned you in?" the skipper said. He started to laugh.

"I'd do the same for my kid, if I ever had to," he said, and the look in his eyes took the smile from the skipper's face.

That night we anchored not far from the village of Tununak. The wind whipped down from cliffs, beating the water into froth. No one was herring fishing yet. The fish camp site was still deep in ice. But we saw local men out in skiffs when the wind died. They said they were seal hunting. Their village was iced in too.

Two days later, the company sent us on again, to Bezboro Island in Norton Sound. The ice had cleared. It was open water all the way north. But no charts were available for those waters. "Local Knowledge Only" was written on the broad blank margins of the coast on the few maps we did have.

We pulled in behind the island just before dawn, in the strangely colored rose and gold of an Arctic spring. Bezboro was narrow and steep, like a knife-edge rising from the sea. Talus and scree trailed down from the central peak. Elsewhere lay tundra and a few dwarf willow bent double by the prevailing wind. Past the island the sea dissolved into wild gray. There was no land beyond until Asia.

People from Shaktoolik called that night on the radio. They made talk, politely, telling us what animals they'd seen recently and what the winter was like. Some were out hunting for belugas. In winter, they hand-lined for king crab, they said. Through summer there was fishing along the coast and berry picking.

Next day I walked the island ridge, high on tundra uplands alive with birds. I was so high that when I saw whales surfacing below me and saw them blow, a long beat passed before I heard their breaths. Snow clung to the ribs and hollows of the island. But here and there, pussy willows bloomed, the tiny frost of ruby on their gray down hypnotic to my color-starved eyes.

That night the men built a bonfire, using waste oil rags as a fire starter, on a strand of gravel jutting from the steep shore of the island. Meanwhile, I looked for bones along the tideline. A few wildflowers blew on the spit, though their leaves were not yet out; bright catkins, salvia with lavender spires, and blue pasque flowers.

After a while I wandered back to the fire. The men were drinking beer and telling stories. Nick, made introspective by the fire, told one that seemed to be something he thought of often but rarely spoke of. When he was nineteen, his best friend was killed. It was the spring they would have graduated. His friend got drunk and stood on the railroad tracks on a dare. He didn't jump out of the way quite fast enough.

"It changed me," Nick said. "It scared me straight, for one thing. But I never feel that happy any more, the way I used to. I kind of thought being young was supposed to last a little longer than it did."

The four of us stared at the dying fire, watching tongues of light appear and disappear and the dull glow of its central embers. Tony was drinking hard, sucking whiskey from a little flask. I saw the skipper notice what was happening and start to gather us up. He told me softly he was worried about getting Tony from the skiff onto the boat.

"I don't want any drownings."

Nick did not want to leave.

"Already?" he said, but we went anyway. Back onboard we went our separate ways. But Nick sat in the center of the galley, trying to hold us each in talk as we passed. The journey was wearing him down.

On a cold, gray, and windy night, the herring began to spawn at last. We heard the people of Shaktoolik had begun fishing. We could hear the steady murmur of voices on VHFs almost too far away to hear. We headed out to them, a light rain falling, and took scattered deliveries through the day and night and into the following day. By nightfall on the third night, when fishing closed, the fishermen were strung out behind us waiting to deliver, a long line of open skiffs filled with families, come from the village out to the herring. They passed lines boat to boat to moor themselves behind the *Jamie D.* Each delivery was small. At first they waited patiently in the bottom of their boats, sitting with their own backs to the wind, hoods pulled over their heads, a pile of gillnet in each boat, and a sea of the silvery backs of fish.

But our pump was slow, and the weather was picking up. One by one, the fishermen made their way along the boats and over the side of the *Jamie D*, into the galley to warm up. In to where I wrote fish tickets for each boat, straining to hear the numbers Chris shouted to me as the fish pump bucked and clanged. Tony, on top of the pump, struggled to shove the fish forward as they fell, to keep them flowing. Wind and rain beat in his face. He squinted against them. His hands looked icy cold. Twice I climbed up to help him. The herring were so ripe, they spawned as they fell, globs of bright red roe, elastic on the outside, tough, and sticking to almost anything.

Together, we pushed the fish along with shovels, sweating despite the cold and our cold hands, the cold rain and sweat running down our backs. Our arms burned. Exhausted, hungry, I grabbed a chunk of roe and bit into it. It tasted like the sea—tough, salt, marine, like a memory of long ago.

Then the skipper called me back to do fish tickets. I scrambled down the ladder once more. The galley now was full of strangers, quiet people shoulder to shoulder, shy, but too cold to go back out on deck. They laughed with each other, though not with me. I saw a little kid hunched against the wall, his sweatshirt wringing wet. He let me put it in the dryer. Soon, they all passed me wet outer garments. And they were hungry. I filled the stove with pots. We had spaghetti. We were all so tired, after three days without sleep, a hallucinatory tiredness bright with the smell of herring and the sea, the clang of metal, and those laughing voices.

Someone was telling me about his son, who'd shot himself the year before. Someone was writing poetry in the galley, on a scrap of paper he borrowed from the fish ticket book.

I saw the sour face of the other deckhand. Tony's weary eyes. Heard the skipper's harsh, determined shout as he forced the failing pump to work. In the cold dawn, the last boat slipped away. Three days in, and the season was over. I guessed I had fed eighty people. The skipper scolded me for that, but he didn't understand what we'd shared as we waited in the night, as the herring spawned and all around animals fed.

The tenders never went to Norton Sound again. Two years later, Tony died, drowned on a summer night in a capsized skiff. I heard they found his body. I never knew his son. I walked the shore near where it happened, thinking of him. Thinking of all of us that night on the herring grounds. How it had been, how little time it lasted. It was a strange kind of peace to think about it, and a strange kind of grief for a friend.

I don't know where the years have gone or what became of the place we shared. It may be herring still spawn there in the spring. They must be sweet.

Bathurst Inlet, Nunavut

◆

Summer 2010

Inuksiut, stones piled in human shapes, marked the bare tundra along the coast. Long ago, people from another time laid them in place to frighten caribou so they would crowd together, passing close by hidden hunters. I thought it eerie to see them here, stark against the Arctic sky.

I was alone, kayaking on the coast of Nunavut, in the Canadian Arctic. Earlier that spring, I'd written villages along the coast, trying to find a way to travel north to the Northwest Passage. A woman wrote back to me from Bathurst Inlet and offered to sell me space on their spring cargo flight. She offered, too, to loan me her kayak, so I would not use space on the plane for mine.

I drove north to Yellowknife on gravel roads—the Alaska Highway and up the Liard, two-lane highways rutted with potholes and permafrost heaves. Entering the Northwest Territories. I carried gas cans strapped to the roof rack. When I stopped, horseflies attacked in droves. Mosquitoes crowded so thick it was hard to breathe.

I camped in Watson Lake, Liard, Fort Providence. I'd traveled here before as a child. I remembered oars creaking as they caught the water. Sun hot on an old lifejacket, rose-colored rocks, and blue water. I was three years old, in the Northwest Territories, crossing Great Slave Lake with my family. It was my first memory, from so long ago now. My parents had taken me and my older sister to spend a summer in the wild, like so many others drifting in from elsewhere. For my parents, it had been simple joy in exploration and camp life on the water. For me now, perhaps, it was something stranger: an unfulfillable dream or an erasure.

Crossing the Mackenzie River, I spent a night camped near a mission graveyard. The stones were old, half-buried in wild roses. Some carried the names of men and women from the region. Others marked the graves of mission sisters born in France who died here far from home. I wondered what had called them here, and what had kept them. It seemed so lonely. Had they, too, felt that unquiet yearning to strive for farther worlds, for more and larger contact with what they saw as wilderness? And what damage had they wrought by their presence, or what, if any, good?

Yellowknife was bigger than I'd expected, crowded with tourists. No one talked to me but a woman drinking port wine from a bottle behind the gas station; she was leaning on a chain-link fence, cigarette butts at her feet. She did not tell me her name but offered me a sip. I thanked her for her kindness, because that was what it was, though the wine was too sweet and thick on my tongue. I was not sure what to say to her, to ease the sad look in her eyes. Something seemed broken inside her.

I thought of what I knew of the displacement that had followed hard on the heels of outsiders coming to the land. Of the abuse inflicted on the people of this place by other people who looked like me, and I wondered what had happened to this woman, or to her community through the years. Her story was her own; she did not share it with a stranger. Only the wine, and a difficult, brief peace, the generosity of summer in the sun.

I said goodbye to her after a while, walked slowly back to sleep in my car. Next day, I boarded the Twin Otter and flew north over the Barren Grounds, the great expanse of tundra and water that blankets northern Canada. I couldn't see much strapped in the cargo section with my gear and with stacks of food and soda for the village. When the plane landed, cold fresh air rushed in. Half-dazed by Arctic light, I got out onto a landing strip surrounded by strangers. Three or four women, two half-grown girls, a few adult men, and a young boy. Children played at the edge of the landing strip, breaking off to stare.

"Who are you?" one of them asked.

A woman stepped forward and spoke to me. Page, who'd answered my letter. She'd come here decades before from Hudson Bay and chose to remain. The others had grown up at Bathurst Inlet, their ties here stretching back over centuries.

Before the coming of outsiders to the land, Inuit hunters used Bathurst Inlet as a seasonal camp, scattering inland to hunt caribou in summer and moving onto the sea ice to build snow huts in winter. But when a Hudson's Bay trading post was built here, at the mouth of the Burnside River, some of the local hunters settled near the post, building one of the first permanent communities in Nunavut. Now there were a handful of houses and a lodge. That was Bathurst, population nineteen. The previous winter had been the first in living memory when no one wintered there. One of the elders needed oxygen, and people moved with her to the hospital at Cambridge Bay for the winter rather than have her go alone, Page had written me.

Now, some of the men helped me carry my gear from the landing strip. They were quiet, not talking or saying their names, but they seemed glad enough that I was there. I'd worried I would be an intruder.

Page asked me to stay in the lodge that night.

"There've been bears around," she said. "Grizzlies. You should be careful when you're out on the land."

She told me there never used to be so many there. They were moving north with the warming climate. Here, at the edge of their range, they were hungry. That winter, one had broken into the lodge. It ate a five-gallon bucket of Crisco stored in the kitchen.

"That took forever to clean up," she said.

As she talked, I followed her into a large, open room lined with tools of carved ivory and bone. She was a sturdy but lonely seeming woman; she showed me the tools as another woman might have introduced her family. Though they were worn with use, they did not look old. It was as if the worker had stepped out of the room, not long ago, and would return to claim his work at any moment.

The people here were Qinguanmuit. They say Bathurst Inlet was settled first by Thule and Copper Inuit, ancestors of its modern-day inhabitants. Long afterward, when European explorers and traders began to make their way into the Arctic, they came for the most part from the east and west. Here, Bathurst Inlet, the midpoint of the Canadian Arctic coast, became one of the last places in the Western Hemisphere for whites and First Nation peoples to make contact. So isolated, the people here had been protected longer from epidemics and colonization. They kept their own ways.

In the summer of 1821, Sir John Franklin reached Bathurst waters while searching for the Northwest Passage. He and his men descended the Coppermine River from Great Slave Lake, which was then the limit of European geographical knowledge, and traveled east as far as the inlet. They retreated too late in the brief Arctic summer, ascending the Hood River back toward Yellowknife and home. As winter approached, the party split up. Lacking knowledge of the land, many died of cannibalism, murder, and starvation.

Franklin himself survived. Later, he tried again to find the Northwest Passage by sailing west from Hudson Bay. His ships were lost in the ice with all his men. It would be over a century before they were found, their desperate effort to escape remembered by a few Inuit families, who saw their starving march but could not help them. They were hampered by lack of common language, by, perhaps, the cultural arrogance of the whites, and by the sheer fact of too many men in a hungry country.

After Franklin's disastrous journey, searchers for his expeditions traversed the north. Yankee whalers sailed higher into the Arctic; Hudson Bay trappers and voyageurs traveled the rivers. Others came still seeking the Northwest Passage or the North Pole, bringing irrevocable changes to the land. In 1912 two explorers, Harry Radford and Thomas Street, were killed on the sea ice by men from Bathurst, in one of the last open hostilities of the time. Radford struck one of the Inuit men to force "obedience" when he tried to leave the expedition. The other Inuit reacted in self-defense. In the ensuing fight, Street was killed while running for firearms on the sled. Later, Royal Canadian Mounted Police officials came from Hudson Bay to investigate, a journey that covered over five thousand miles by dogsled. The Inuit men involved explained what happened, and charges were not filed. It seemed clear the Inuit men had no choice.

A century after Franklin's lost expedition, in the 1930s, a Catholic mission was established in Bathurst Inlet at the mouth of the Burnside River. The first priest there was a man named Father

Raymond. He became chief doctor through a flu epidemic that killed a quarter of the Bathurst people. In a diary of grief, he wrote of seeing children die, of watching the survivors walk away across the ice, struggling to pull their sleds in decimated groups. One girl, Nuyuk, he'd known all her short life. He described her sinking in the fever, trying helplessly to save her, and her asking, "Father, why must I die and leave this beautiful place?"

He did not have an answer.

Father Raymond stayed at Bathurst Inlet until he contracted tuberculosis and left the north. He died soon afterward in British Columbia. The mission was later deconsecrated and sold. It still stood empty above the village. A retired RCMP official from Yellowknife and his wife bought the trading post in 1969 and ran it as a lodge in partnership with the Kinguanmuit, the Bathurst people. When Page arrived, tents were giving way to tin-roofed houses. There was a school, community space. A movie projector had reached the village.

I knew that through the north First Nations children had often been taken from their parents and sent to schools faraway. That it had left a legacy of abuse. That in a way, as a stranger in the place, Page might have played an ambiguous role. But though she talked of hard times, how it was difficult now for people to remain on the land, the isolation, and changes in the North that came through drugs and alcohol, she did not dwell on sad things but joyful ones—like traveling Outside and smuggling back a pet snake to show the children here. They were so pleased, she said. It seemed to her not long ago. Though it was clear that Page, however bonded with the community, was still to some degree an outsider and always would be.

As we talked, the two girls slipped in to use the satellite internet. Looking up as Page went to make tea, they asked if I wanted to see how they could throat sing. Facing each other, they launched into a strange music, one following the other's lead. It was like nothing I'd ever heard, a song sounding out of deep time, yet the girls themselves were bubbly middle schoolers, their cheeks still round with baby fat, wearing glitter in their hair and pretty jeans.

Finished, suddenly shy, they ran away. I went out to bring my gear inside. The skies had cleared. A slight breeze stirred open water, and wildflowers bloomed brilliant in the grass. Dwarf fireweed, cotton grass, and Arctic poppies. In the distance, the islands of the inlet marched toward the hills, the water between them stirred dark blue. I walked past a handful of small, bare cabins at the mouth of the Burnside River. Mosquitoes whined in the grass, but the breeze was too strong for them to fly. Children exploded past me down the track, running and riding bicycles, hair flying, shouting. They looked so happy, more alive somehow than kids from town.

A VHF radio crackled to life through the open window of one of the cabins. Someone inviting everyone over for tea and bread, over the village channel. I knew they didn't mean me. It made me feel curiously lonely.

On the landing strip, people were gathering again. As I came near, I saw them move together, looking at the far side of the strip. A grizzly climbed out of the grass. A yearling, terribly thin. It rose on its hind legs to get a better look.

Someone shouted. It stopped. Backed up. Moved toward the group again.

Farther down the track, a man yelled, gunning his four-wheeler toward the bear. It disappeared, thrashing through scrub willow out of sight. The people looked at each other. I was glad to be sleeping indoors.

As I turned back to the lodge, a teenage boy caught up to me. He began to speak and broke off, his body language uncontrolled and compulsive, mirroring convulsive thoughts. He seemed deeply disturbed, more so than I'd seen before. I wondered if, in the outer world, someone like him might have been less visible, but here, his family had chosen—could choose—to keep him with them, sheltered by their isolation. Though he was troubled, he was trying hard to talk. I tried to listen.

That night, I woke with an insistent sense something was wrong. In the dim light, I saw the boy. He was standing by the bed, staring at me.

"Please go away," I said.

His face worked miserably. He slipped out. In a moment, I heard him scraping and crying at the window, his face pressed to the pane beside my bed. I got up and blocked the door. I felt so sad, but I couldn't help it. In the morning, I did not tell what had happened. It would have felt like a betrayal of someone's need for contact, too great to be expressed.

I loaded Page's kayak on the shore. It was tiny. I had to leave much of my gear, and in the end, she could not find the spray skirt. But it was enough for me. I left the village paddling into a hard, fresh wind, heading out to waters I'd never seen, past those few isolated houses. Earth and sea alike were shades of blue and lavender; islands dissolved in the distance, into Arctic sky. Though the water slapped up against my kayak, and though I knew that it was dangerous without a spray skirt, I kept going. Nervous, lonely, determined, cold, already a little overwhelmed, and yet oddly happy.

Page had told me to watch for stone circles. "They were tent rings," she said. "Some of them are thousands of years old."

That night, I camped on one of the islands, hoping to avoid the bears. As I pulled in, the keel crunched softly over gravel. The shore was layered deep in stone circles, close-set rings of heavy rock left by the Thule people, and later by Copper Inuit, to weight the edges of their skin tents. Lighter stones lay in circles more widely spaced, left by those longer ago, the makers of the Arctic Small Tool tradition that flourished here thousands of years ago, before its people disappeared. It was utterly plain and seemed unbearably recent, as though the slightest curtain hung between myself and the people who had camped here. And yet we were separated by a gulf of time I couldn't bridge.

I pulled my kayak up and walked the shore looking for a place to pitch my own tent where I would not disturb the patient stones. I saw a ledge where heavier rocks had been laid over the weathered bones of a seal. People here cached animals that way, in the days when sudden shortage meant starvation. Nearer the village, I'd been told, a tall outcrop of rock still smelled of seal oil. The people told me they believed their Bathurst ancestors cached seal fat there, sewn in skin bags and placed high where animals couldn't reach. They'd leave the cache there when they went to hunt caribou inland in the summer months, in case of fatal scarcity when they returned to the coast in the fall. But sometimes the bags leaked a little in the summer heat. And that slow leakage seeped into the stone, so that now, scratching the rocks with a fingertip, you could still catch that long-ago scent from the past.

At last I found a ledge where I could camp. I slept lightly that night, listening half-awake for bears, listening to the silence of the land. I felt a sense of fear, of being a stranger here, and a clear awareness bordering on awe of something greater than myself.

Two days later, I reached Coronation Gulf, where the inlet widened to open water. This was the Northwest Passage Franklin and his men had come so far to see, and had died without crossing. Now, choked with ice and prone to sudden storms, it opened before me.

Blue sky, blue sea, smudged-blue horizon. I floated at its mouth, looking at what seemed the ultimate edge of the world.

In 1906, after Franklin died, Amundsen transited these waters in the *Gjoa*, in what was called the first crossing of the Northwest Passage. But for all those explorers who tried and failed, died or succeeded, there were others who remained unrecognized because they'd always lived here and traveled the coast knowing it not as wilderness but as home. It seemed to me that those who traveled on, seeking a far-off glory, missed the mark. I had to wonder if Franklin thought so, too, if he remembered home at the last and wished he'd never gone away. Or if he wished he understood this northern land as a place more than as a route to conquer.

The wind picked up, building the sea into steep chop. I turned back from Coronation Gulf, to paddle southeast again along the farther shore of Bathurst Inlet. In camp that night, I saw a mother grizzly and her cubs work their way over tundra that lay brilliant green in the endless June light. They, too, looked ragged, thin, and tired. I lay still, hoping they would not see me, listening to the wind race over head stirring the grass and sea. Looked up to see their disappearing backs, working slowly along the shore out of my sight. Even they were more at home here than I.

The following day, I traveled along cliffs. Late in the day, the wind rose swiftly, from a steady breeze to fierce gusts heated over the bare rocks and spilling down to where I struggled in my inadequate kayak. Suddenly, the water smoked white in spray, over blue wind chop. I could not land; the shoreline was too steep.

Far ahead, I could see the shelving rock of a point. I knew I had to reach it. Deep down inside, everything became quite still. I balanced, stroke by stroke, the waves slapping steeply up into the well of the kayak. I knew that if I swamped I would probably die. I was alone, too far from home.

Leaning against the wind, I began to sing. This song, too, came out of deep time, though a different place, a different land. I sang children's songs to the howling sea. I would rather have had a different song, but it helped.

I wonder if my fear was some small part of how the others felt, Franklin when his ships were wrecked, responsible for his men and knowing no help would come; the European men themselves, all too far from home; and even perhaps the skilled, intelligent hunters of this place. They too died of exposure sometimes, or starvation when the game did not come. They, too, may have known that sense of helplessness. Of being in a world too large.

Stroke by stroke, I neared the shelving rock, braced against the knifing wind. My wrists burned with the strain. Inches of ice-cold water filled the boat. But I reached the landing and rolled ashore. For a moment I just breathed.

I knew I couldn't rest for long. I was too cold. I dragged the kayak far up the rock, secured it, and stripped off my wet clothes. Pulled on dry long johns, ate a handful of candy for warmth, and set my tent up in a crack in the rocks, half-protected from the wind.

Next, I looked for fresh water in the hollows of the rocks, climbing the ridge and peering down. I had often had trouble finding drinking water, so much of it was salty here. I knew I couldn't launch again if I failed. But at last, I saw a deep pool, arms-length down between two rocks. I dipped a panful, lying on my belly. Set it to boil, beginning suddenly to enjoy the dailiness of these small tasks, making a home on barren rock, bringing comfort out of the cold land. That night I slept deeply, and woke to a glorious dawn, windless, scrubbed clean of fear and memory, full of gratitude to be alive.

In weeks to come, I traveled farther along the shore of Bathurst Inlet. I saw caribou leaning into the wind. Crystals in the cliffs colored amethyst and rose, stromatolites marking the rocks, and wildflowers on the shore. I came upon a human skeleton laid out on stone, in a precontact burial. The place was not marked but remembered by the people here. A handful of weathering bones under the sky, in the loveliest place I'd ever seen. In the end, I lost at last something of the aching sense of fear and displacement that followed me in the early days here and found instead a weary sense of peace.

At the end of July, after a month on the water, I paddled back to the village. When I reached the shore, I saw the boy again at the landing strip. He had a rash on his face now. His mother sat a little to the side. I saw her call him over and smear some ointment on his skin. I saw the look in her eyes, so loving that I turned away. So raw and tender, beautiful and sad, something no stranger like me could understand.

But the village looked different to me now, a refuge rather than an outpost. That night I climbed the slope behind the lodge. I could see the route Franklin had taken toward the Hood River. The inlet shone blue where once the villagers had gone in single file across the ice after the epidemic. Out there, Radford and Street had died; here a people had made a home living in a place that was harsh but everything to them, both the bitter and the sweet. Others had chosen, too, to stay. It wasn't long ago. Not long at all.

Soon after, I caught the plane to Yellowknife. I watched Bathurst Inlet fade behind me, its tiny, bright cabins by the river growing smaller until they passed from sight. I felt the longing that bound these people to this place and unexpected sorrow that I would not see it again. I knew I half-wished that I could stay. And I wondered if the others had felt the same.

On the *Tiglax*

◆

Summer 2014

We arrived at Attu just before dawn, in a clear, deep inlet ringed with golden grass. I went out on the bow to drop the anchor. Overhead, the sky turned faint blue, the highest clouds already touched with light. It was so quiet, as if the island held its breath.

The rumble of the anchor chain falling broke the stillness. The first mate backed the boat down on the chain, laying it out. A shackle, two, three. When he nodded, I braked the chain, dogged it, and reset the winch. Then everything was still again, except for the faint gabble of geese waking up somewhere on shore.

That summer I worked as able seaman on the *Tiglax*, a Fish and Wildlife vessel that spent its summers in the Aleutians running surveys for the Maritime Refuge along the Aleutian chain. I had joined it at Adak three days before. We ran from there to Attu, far out at sea, across the international date line from the rest of Alaska.

A thousand miles down the Aleutian Chain, Attu was formed by lava rising under the sea, at the subduction zone where the Pacific Plate dives into the Aleutian Trench. The islands lie between the mile-deep waters of the trench, and the shallower, warmer Bering Sea. Fogs billow up out of the summer ocean and hang above the surface for days. There are sudden currents, violent winds. An immensity of distance separates each island from the world.

My shift was over at 6:00 a.m. But I stayed to watch as the sun came up. Attu has been uninhabited since its Unangan occupants were captured by the Japanese and taken to Japan at the start of World War II. They spent the war in internment camps there, housed twenty to a room in buildings with rotting floors. More than a third died, lacking food, clean water, and basic medical care. After the war, the survivors from Attu were sent back to the United States, but the American government did not take them back to Attu. Instead, perhaps for financial reasons, perhaps because so few Attuans had survived, or perhaps in the false belief one island was much like another, US officials consolidated villages and settled the people of Attu farther up the chain with those who'd been interned by the United States in Southeast Alaska. The Attuans never saw their island again.

Attu, though, is like nowhere else on earth. The wind blows and the grass ripples until the island seems alive. Seabirds spill from the cliffs like a river, swinging back up high and spilling again. No other species claims the land. Standing on deck, I wondered if the villagers had broken hearts missing this island. Once gone, how could they ever return?

Late morning, the *Tiglax* idled out of the harbor, to drop the scientists once they readied their gear. I stood on deck as the other deckhand navigated the near-shore rocks in the skiff, looking for a place where he could set the scientists onshore.

Sea lions have declined rapidly in the Aleutians, no one quite knows why. They could be the victims of some larger predator, such as transient orcas or sleeper sharks, which have in turn seen their original food source become less abundant. They could be early casualties of ocean changes linked to a warming climate. Or, they could be starving. Deepwater trawlers frequent the area in winter, and though their bycatch quotas are capped, those quotas appear high enough to have an impact down the chain. These biologists hoped the cameras would offer data on sea lion haul-outs that were inaccessible to study for most of the year. They were also looking for animals that had been branded as pups, to gauge survival rates and distribution of adults.

Two nights later, we stopped at Agattu, where the sea hollowed out the cliffs into caves. The skipper, Billy, launched two skiffs, and drove one, telling me to follow. He stood solidly at the tiller of his skiff, a small, tough man with bright, dark eyes holding the far-off look of those too long alone with sky and sea. The Aleutian stare. Perhaps he had too much bravado, having seen too much. He headed straight into the mouth of a sea cave. I followed through the entrance where the swells sucked and rose against the cliffs, into darkness and deep water.

On the far side, we came out of the passage into a well in the rock. Cliffs rose on all sides, spilling birds. Incoming ripples slapped at the foot of the cliffs as Billy drifted with his crew. I kept my eyes on the water, trying to control my skiff.

When Billy swung his boat around and headed out, I followed. The tunnel narrowed. Inside the mouth, I saw a swell larger than the rest rising at us. It was too late to turn, and there was nowhere to run. The wave broke as we saw it, steepened by the constricting walls.

"Go Go GO!" one of the men shouted.

I gunned the throttle, running straight at the face of the breaker, understanding what he meant because there was no possible other option. The boat seemed to respond impossibly slowly. Four of the men flung themselves on the bow, weighting it down, as the boat rose nearly vertically up the face of the wave and teetered for a moment on the brink. I could see the silver line of the peak just at the bow. It scratched itself into my memory, seeming to take forever to fall.

Then the crest swept past. The bow dropped. The next wave came, smaller than the first, and we were through the cave, into open water. Billy waited just outside the break. I gave him a thumbs-up, but my hands shook. He nodded and passed on down the coast. I followed. There was nothing else I could do.

"I just wanted to see if you guys had drowned," was all he said.

Next day, I took the men ashore near a sea lion haul-out. When we arrived, the surf was breaking high. As I'd been told, I drove in fast, straight through the surf, the rocks, the kelp, and the current, riding the crest of a wave behind the break. When we struck the beach, I jumped out into the surf and stood thigh-deep, struggling to hold the boat.

"Never let it get broadside to the wave," Billy had told me. "That's when you'll roll it or swamp for sure."

I did my best. The scientists scrambled over the bow and made a chain, passing gear to offload the boat. When it was empty, we shoved it through the surf. But I could not get the outboard to fire. I washed backward almost onto the shore before the motor kicked and thrust my way off again, thinking, "Jesus Christ."

Outside the break, I sheltered from the swell behind a reef, waiting for the scientists to complete their work. From the cliffs above, birds spilled wildly down, plummeting to spatter on the surface of the water. Auklets. Murres. Terns. They rode the wind high in drifting circles, but when they tumbled from their cliff-side nests, they passed like meteorites. Puffins nested below slopes where the grass grew so thick and tall it reached over my head.

The body of a sea lion lay on shore, its blonde hide gashed with bloody wounds. The males fight fiercely over harem space and sometimes kill each other or crush the smaller females. Billy said he'd seen them with entrails hanging, still alive. I could hear them huffing behind me in the water as I drifted, waiting. I worried. Every now and then, a sea lion will grab a person.

Next day, we woke to fogbanks on the water. Billy dropped me in the skiff to set the scientists ashore on a handful of rocks hammered by surf. The ship would patrol the area looking for orcas for a tagging study during the hours the other scientists were onshore.

"There's no good place to tie up," he told me. "You'll have to wait offshore in the skiff again."

"Just keep your radio on," he added. "I'll come back for you. And if you get lost in the fog, try to keep moving. That way I'll pick you up on the radar."

Nearing the shore in the skiff, I found a rock face where the water rose and fell without surging and offloaded the others to the shore. Then I did as Billy said. I found a thick bed of drifting kelp and ran straight into it. The kelp deadened the swell as it passed. The boat rocked like a sea otter in clear, still water. I looked down at the leaves swaying far under the boat. The fog settled, so I could see only the ghost of the shore. But the kelp held me, drifting in a slow arc as the sea lion biologists did their work.

After an hour, I'd passed gently a little down the shore. I worked my way out of the kelp, ran up-current in open water, and worked my way back in again, taking care not to let the outboard overheat. The shore crew called me late in the afternoon. Passing out of sight of the island, we found the *Tiglax* and were again in fog so thick you could see only the flat, gray water on each side of the keel, a wall of mist against the wheelhouse windows.

Though Unangan people have lived there thousands of years, Europeans did not see the Aleutian Islands until 1741, when the Russian explorer Vitus Bering led an expedition east from Kamchatka on the *St. Peter*. They made landfall at Kayak Island on the gulf coast of Alaska. There, the naturalist, Georg Steller, was allowed to go ashore for a few hours, the first non-native to reach Alaskan soil. He saw a bird, now called Steller's jay, which he recognized as related to the American blue jay. It was proof they had indeed reached North America.

On the return voyage, the crew sickened with scurvy. With most of the men already dead or dying, Bering's ship wrecked in fog on the Komandorski Islands, halfway to Russia. Bering himself died soon after. The remaining men wintered on the islands in huts built of the ship's timbers. Foxes bedeviled them, stealing food and even chewing on their feet. Steller suffered like the rest but also used the time to record the fauna of those islands, including Steller's sea cow, a sirenian unique to those islands.

At last, in the spring, the men escaped by building a lifeboat of wood scavenged from the wrecked *St. Peter*. Steller lived to carry his notes back to Russia, but he died soon afterward in Siberia, exiled for supposed revolutionary sympathies. Nevertheless, the book he wrote, *On the Beasts of the Sea*, contains the first descriptions of flora and fauna in the Aleutians. It was later used by explorers like James Cook and by the Russian fur traders.

In the years after Bering's expedition, traders first ventured to the Aleutians, lured by the tales of islands of sea otter and by the richness of the furs brought back by Bering's men. In a few years, they devastated sea otter populations and Unangan villages alike and drove the Steller's sea cow to extinction. They enslaved Unangan men and forced them to hunt sea otter. Many Unangan died; others were shot as sport. Those years are remembered in the place-names of the islands. Massacre Bay. Murder Point. There are skulls still buried in the grass, on the rock-bound shores past where we rode day after day, balanced on tiptoes to the sway of the boat, watching ghosts in the fog.

But when the fog lifted, the land was so beautiful. Albatross scudded down foam-streaked seas. They dipped first one wing, then the other, skimming on their stiff points just above the cresting seas, never quite touching. In June there came a day so quiet, we passed through great flocks of ocean birds settled on the water. It was too calm for them to ride the wind; even the albatross rested on the surface. The sea, perfectly blue, reflected the perfect blue of the sky. Black-footed and Laysan albatross. A great bird with a head dusted lightly sunshine yellow, a short-tailed albatross rocking slowly on the water.

Northeast, up the Aleutian chain, we dropped anchor at Kiska. The skipper and I went ashore. Up close, the grass that looked so green shone bright with flowers, blue and pink and yellow. Fireweed and lupine, buttercup and wild geranium, bitter yarrow and wild beach pea.

In World War II, during the summer of 1942, when Japanese troops invaded the Aleutian Islands, they dug tunnels here on Kiska to withstand bombardment. They had stayed here through an Aleutian winter and slipped away under cover of fog in the spring of 1943. Days later, US ground troops arrived, effectively ending the war in the Aleutians, though it was years before the Unangan people were allowed to return. Even here, in these far-off islands, traces remained of World War II's ragged demolition of the earth, in pursuit of what gain.

The skipper knew where to find those tunnels still. I followed him up the shore past part of a military tank rusting at the water's edge, and we veered off through dense grass, inland along a steep ravine.

"It must be here somewhere," he said. Parting the grass, he found an opening in the earth, scarcely wide enough for him to work his shoulders through. He dropped into it, out of sight. I followed him, falling into darkness.

The skipper had a flashlight. I did not. I kept my hand on his elbow to guide my steps, the light from his flashlight shadowed by his shoulders. It was so absolutely dark, it seemed to press against my eyes. The walls of the tunnel shed dirt under my fingertips, and reaching up, I could feel the ceiling just over our heads. But I trusted him.

He stopped abruptly where the tunnel widened, deep under the mountain, and played his light over the rough ceiling and walls. A worn boot lay against the wall, crumbling slowly into dust. Other than that, the room was still. Neither of us had anything to say. The war seemed so near, so lonely, wasteful, and sad, though the men that sheltered here had all perhaps been dead for years now, age catching those who escaped the war itself. The Japanese who'd built the tunnels, and who crouched in them unable to retreat, were for the most part teenagers. But they too were gone.

From Kiska, the boat headed north again. Petrels fluttered against the boat and beat at the windows. They skittered along the unfamiliar steel until they found a corner in which to crouch, where they became trapped because they could not spread their wings. I walked the decks until I found them, warmed them in my hands and lightly put them back into the sky again. Once, I failed to catch one in time. I saw it fall from the side of the boat, too cold to spread its wings, and tumble over, drowning, in our wake. How sharp a minor memory can be, that failure of mine to reach it in time.

"Next time," Billy said, "keep it in your sweatshirt until your blood warms it enough it can move." A simple instruction. "I've done it many times."

Anchoring at strange islands in the dark, I heard the cries of birds on unseen heights. But some few islands were silent. Before World War II, foxes had been introduced to these islands. They were raised for fur, for markets back East, and bred here without natural predators, which allowed them to wreak havoc among the birds. There were few cliffs the foxes could not climb to steal eggs. The birds had never known a land-based predator. But in the '90s, the foxes were trapped out on many islands, as part of a government project, and on those islands the birds had reclaimed the cliffs. Even in the dark, I could tell if there were foxes on an island, from the sound of the birds, the ringing clamor of voices in the night.

In daylight, we passed an island, Kasatochi, which erupted five years before. It had been blanketed in flows of hot ash over a hundred feet deep in places. Now, years later, the island was still stark gray, a few faint lines of grass just beginning to take root. We idled past the shore, caked with ash, extended far outside its earlier boundaries by pyroclastic flows. The skipper told me the auklets had come back every year after the eruption and nested in the same sites each spring, though the nest sites were buried deep.

"It was years before they raised chicks there again," he said. Yet they'd tried every spring, a long-lived bird with inescapable fidelity to place. That was how the islands worked. The lushness of the grass itself was testament to the recurring cycle of eruptions. In the thickness of the grass, too, birds died, caught in a green tangle, and their bones fertilized the ever-moving islands.

Late at night, we saw a faint sliver of lights on Amchitka, where the naval base was. The first in many nights.

"Those folks must be so lonely," Billy said. "They don't belong, not like the Aleuts did."

Aside from the base, Amchitka is uninhabited. The island was used as a nuclear test site by the United States. Three nuclear warheads were detonated here, including a five-megaton bomb in 1971. The force of that bomb cracked the freshwater lens of the island. Poison leached into the soil, and into the eyries of birds, and the seawater that washed its shores. Amchitka still has abnormally high radiation levels. Wild as it seemed in passing, it had been changed by man.

"That one, at least, will never be the same."

But already, it was falling in our wake.

In the Islands of the Four Mountains we searched for transient orcas. We carried a team now that hoped to tag them. Transient, flesh-eating orcas split from the resident, fish-eating phenotype perhaps thousands of years ago. Though visually, they are nearly identical, their languages and hunting cultures are nothing alike, and they never interbreed. Little is known about those that live in the Aleutians except that they are disappearing. Perhaps their food sources have shrunk too much. Perhaps some other cause is at fault. Or perhaps, like so many other things, it is a death by papercut, of a thousand little things, small changes, piling up to make life just too difficult.

The whale researchers talked of their quest in semi-mystical terms, speaking of how to feel the difference between resident and transient in words that made Billy scoff. And yet, I had a sneaking sympathy for them. Their task was difficult, perhaps impossible: tagging wild transient orcas. And yet it mattered enough to them to try; it was the only chance they saw to understand their lives enough to save them.

We never saw a transient pod, though we patrolled for a long time. Not enough is known of where they frequent, only that they exist. Meanwhile the fog came down again, heavy as a blanket, closing out the world. The whales we saw were resident orcas, fish-eaters, conditioned to a ready supply of bait from long-liners. One followed for a long time at our stern, nosing up to us in expectation of a meal. It had learned the engine sound of a boat slowing to lay gear and learned to run for it, like trash feeders everywhere. Long-liners hate orcas and often try to outwit them, but what can they do? There are not as many fish as there once were.

Meanwhile, the whale huffed and rose at our stern, begging for food. It made me sad. Later, a mother and calf drifted alongside. We killed the motor and drifted with them for a time. They came so close, they all but rubbed against the boat, breathing, offering strange kinship. It took no imagination to believe that they were seeking company from our vessel, even now. It tore my heart to see it, and yet, too, it offered a possibility of redemption. Of looking across some gulf, to feel a kinship for another being. To reach out to it.

Past Kasatochi, we headed northeast. We saw a plume of steam coming from Pavlof Volcano. Eroding islands. At Bogoslof, fur seals watched us approach, snaking slim bodies out of the water, diving, and splashing up alongside the boat. The island belonged entirely to the seals, a world that humanity seemed not to penetrate.

Buldir, home of the birds. At Chirikof, feral cattle brought in by white settlers trampled the grass. Abandoned villages in the Shumagins. Sea wrack and stone. Climbing up Aiktak, grass closed overhead. I felt a brief panic. And then, leaning over the cliff edge, I peered into dizzying depths below, where paint-bright puffins wheeled and turned, falling from their nests into clear air.

At Sand Point, we picked up four teenagers who rode with us for a time. One girl, red-haired, edgy, and fierce, told of fights and sadness in her town. For all its isolated loveliness, drug problems, violence, and broken homes were ordinary to her, the heartbreaking fallout from years of cruelty, of colonization. That legacy is very slow to fade.

Another girl, who smiled but seldom spoke, had a gift for plants and an understanding of the island we couldn't match. A gentle teenager, with a broad, kind face, she followed the scientists at a distance when they went ashore, watching, now and then softly telling the things she knew. She teased us, too, once she knew us better, about the way we pronounced *Tiglax*, the Unangan word for "eagle." The way she said it sounded so beautiful. We couldn't mimic it. Our gestures fell short; we did not truly understand, though we tried. The islands withheld themselves from us as strangers still.

I left the boat in late August, my season done. Before I left, we spent a day on shore in Unalaska. I walked over orange seaweed with its acrid smell and blue mussels wet under a rainy sky. Sea otter drifted in the wrack offshore. The wind kept blowing, shaking water and grass.

When Unangan people failed to return from the sea, their grieving families said, "They found another island." Long ago, here, it was a life so hard, half of older women turned blind. And yet, happiness sings from the old stories, a rich happiness in memories of long ago, before the islands were despoiled. I had to wonder, if we were now on the right track, seeking comfort at all costs. What if comfort does not lead to grace?

And yet. And yet.

For a time, an Arctic fox followed me, its clever, queer, uncanny eyes watching each time I looked back. In Bering's time, the men grew so wild they sometimes tortured foxes to death, maddened by loneliness and rain and snow.

I thought about that, and all the rest of it. The buried tanks and shipwrecks, the holes on Kiska where Japanese soldiers waited, longing to go home, while bombs rattled on the earth outside. I thought about the bones of murdered Unangan in the grass, the birds that wheel and turn and come and go. Sea lions rocking in their beds of kelp, disappearing one by one. Out there for months, you could feel yourself begin to change. The birds never stopped rising and falling, and the wind did not stop. It seemed more real than real, and then nothing was real but the sea itself, the sky, and the weathering stone of a place apart.

On the Pacific Ocean

◆

Summer and Fall 2017

At night the men fished for halibut on the *Tiglax*, anchored near pinnacles where the rock dropped off steeply underwater from peaks green with grass, streaked white with bird droppings. A long silence, the lines cutting down through opaque water. Then the sudden, light vibration, the plucked string, as a halibut mouthed and took the bait. The heavy haul of living weight up to the surface, dull thud of a club, and then the broad, white-bellied fish flapping to its death on the blood-washed deck. Its wry mouth puckering, and tiny, heavy-lidded eyes closing slowly . . . opening . . . closing again. Stiffening. It never took long to kill them; they were so small.

Inside the stern door, a record hung on the wall of halibut weights, the heaviest for each season. It stretched back decades, covering all the many years these men had run this boat for the US Fish and Wildlife Service. But each year the weights were lighter. The large, old fish were largely gone from the Aleutians. Long-liners and commercial fishermen reported also that catches were shrinking, from overfishing perhaps, or from something else, some deep change in ocean chemistry or temperature. Whatever the root cause, the halibut were fewer and smaller now. It made us wonder.

Years later I worked on an oceanographic cruise, a research ship running across the Pacific from Tahiti to Valparaiso, Chile, then down to Punta Arenas in the Straits of Magellan. We crossed the Pacific Gyre, the point in the ocean farthest from any land. Pitcairn Island, Easter Island lay like rumors to our north. Nothing broke the far, pure sweep of the horizon for weeks on end. Only the golden bubble of the sun at dawn and dark, casting light across the ruled shadows of the sea.

We were conducting CTD casts, measuring conductivity, temperature, and depth at set times throughout the day and night as we ran along the thirty-second parallel. Each instrument cast, full ocean depth, took hours. I stood in the open door of the Baltic Room alone, my job to mind the wire and instruments. Tied to the wall with a lifeline at my feet, through the launch door, the ocean rose and fell, swelled and rose and sank. The water seemed transparent deep down, so unproductive of any life. I saw no birds. No ocean life, past the scattered flying fish of Tahiti, and now and then a wandering albatross.

Yet even there, one night, I saw the distant lights of a strange vessel, two weeks out from any land. And saw when day broke over our port bow, a Chinese long-liner laying gear. A near-derelict boat, its once-white steel streaked with rust, listing heavily, and with a listless, ragged crew. So far from home, and even here fishing the farthest corners of the globe.

The water was still so clear, the brightest blue, turquoise where the sun struck it. I remember the color of light through a wave mounting overhead to shatter on the steel wall of the ship. Warm and salty ocean washing over me. And the stars by night, so brilliant overhead. The Southern Cross hanging over our starboard bow. Sometimes the full-bodied moon drowned out even the ship's lights. I'd stand on the bow, shift over at midnight, and feel myself swing through the watches of the night.

Nearing Chile, the water changed, growing opaque steel gray as we approached the Humboldt Current. Its scent changed from the wide, clean smell of open ocean to something brinier, more intimate, more marine. Coastal water, frigid now when seas broke over me. I wore heavy gloves on deck, a Mustang jacket, and still shivered through my watch.

Birds followed us again as the water grew richer, upwelling from the Atacama Trench, and once I saw a Juan Fernández fur seal. It was so like our fur seals in the north but tiny, an odd, shy, acrobatic clown in the water, tumbling solitary about our ship for hours on end. I watched for hours. And when suddenly it was gone, I felt abandoned, alone on the deck of that great ship. As alone as we might be on an empty ocean, if all the fish were gone for good.

Still for now, there were others in the sea. Almost to Valparaiso, mountains already smudging the horizon that had been pure blue sky for so many days, sea lions came out and escorted us into port. I sat and listened to their heavy breaths as if home again, after too long. I felt as if I'd journeyed to a star.

Salvadors at Seal River

◆

July 2013

The beach, backed with silty dunes, swept in a long curve before us. To the east, breakers crashed against this last outpost of land. Icebergs carried down from the glacier scattered along the bank, where swift river water churned into the oncoming tide. At the edge of the sea, where river and tide tore together reshaping the shore, lay the wreck we had come to find.

It lay upright, though breakers stove in the hold. A tug and an eighty-foot barge torn apart and tossed onto the tideline. Two days before, the skipper tried to make a landing in the river mouth, coming in to pick up debris scattered by the Japanese tsunami. The river current proved too strong for his vessel, and the barge spun sideways down the shore until the breakers caught it, tossing it back to land. The tug broke free, and the incoming river windmilled it.

The skipper and his crew tried to jump to safety. The deckhand made it, but the skipper fell short. He could not catch his footing. Undertow carried him backward under the pounding hull. The man who'd waited there to load the barge waded into the surf and caught the skipper by the hair as he went down.

His rescuer dragged him soaked on shore, to wait for help. The boats were past saving. But that night a salvage crew went out to stabilize the situation, recover the fuel, and attempt to refloat the wrecks.

The leader of the crew, Andy, now pulled his ATV up alongside the tug.

"Jump off," he said.

I slid from the rack as other ATVs came up behind us carrying five men, the rest of the salvage crew from Cordova. They'd spent the first night sleeping on the shore. I'd flown in the next morning on a supply plane, hired by chance to be their cook as I walked past their warehouse. Now we had access to an empty lodge ten miles down the shore and these ATVs.

Here, the gulf waters broke against a long, dynamic shore, backed by the upheaval of the Wrangell Mountains. To the east lay the shallow, tidal islands of Copper River Delta, to the west no human settlements until Yakutat. Inland lay the Bering Ice Field, largest in North America. Every year the Bering Glacier pours meltwater into the Gulf of Alaska, and with the recent warm summers that amount was increasing, eroding banks, stripping rock, and washing mountains to the sea.

It was a lonely place. There were no other human traces for miles, only the tracks of bear and wolves. But the men knew what they were doing. Now the five of them scattered around the wrecks. Bill, Steve, Andy, Ardy, Mark. They climbed aboard, I followed. The galley floor was covered with broken glass, sand, things flung against the wall. Wet food, books, clothes. Over everything the smell of ruin.

I'd known the boat before, known the people here. It chilled me now to see it lying so broken. It might have happened to any of us.

Quietly, I began to clean. The few things that could be dried and rescued, I set aside. But other things had to be flung away. I couldn't save them, the wrecked pieces of someone else's life. The men worked until nightfall securing the tug and barge against the tide. We rode back to the lodge crouched against the cold. When we reached it, they smoked under the eaves, out of the rain.

Next morning, we headed out again just after dawn. Low tide. The wrecks had shifted in the night. Andy asked me to shovel sand out of the barge, crouched in spaces too small for the men. It was heavy work, the packed sand half water and hard to shovel out. But the more we cleared, the more chance the barge could float. Meanwhile, Bill built a patch where the stern pontoon had torn away.

We dug a deep trench on the shore above the wrecks. Andy buried a log in it, running a line from it to the barge. A deadman, he called it, a way to moor the barge. The sand was so loose, it shifted day by day as the river and tide tore at it, but the drag of the deadman would still hold the boat.

Part of the barge had torn away and lay some distance off. The men dragged it in with a winch and tried to secure it to the wreck. But the tide had turned, rising across the river mouth. Suddenly, breakers slammed into the boat, as the water rose enough to cross the bar. The torn sheets of aluminum buckled under the force. Over the clanging metal and the sea, I heard shouting. Andy tried to throw a line around the broken piece, to secure it. I could see worry in his eyes. The others gathered by him. At the last moment before we had to run, he caught the piece and made it fast.

"Let's get the hell out of here," he said. We leaped ashore.

Next day they ran the anchors out to secure the barge. The chain was wrapped around an anchor drum that could not move without power. We crouched, one on each side of the drum, passing the chain back and forth to each other. Heavy work, but it made me happy. I'd never worked with men like these.

That night the breakers beat Bill's patch in. He had it all to do again. Again, I hauled damp sand out of the voids to empty the broken hull. Bill tried to flatten the edges of torn aluminum to bolt down the patch, filling the cracks with spray foam. It was difficult work, conducted in frustration that the first patch failed. But half-way through, he stopped to tell me of another job they'd worked the spring before. Like this, they'd been too pressed for time to stop to eat. Anyway, he said, Andy never stopped for food. That wreck had been on the coast near here, an old wooden tender that went ashore and had broken up after it lost steering, and the crew abandoned it. When the men reached it, it was partly awash too. Bill worked in the engine room, fighting the tide that rose around him.

"Hungry as I've ever been," he said.

The boat had been awash with lost possessions: tools and clothes. In the brackish water of the engine room, he saw a can of lemon frosting float past. He grabbed it, tore the lid off, and wolfed it down, eating it straight with filthy hands. Telling the story now, he laughed, good cheer returning.

Next morning a storm rolled in. Wind-bound, we could not leave the lodge. The men slept and talked. Andy spent hours on the satellite phone with his wife, Seawan, who ran the business back in town, and with insurance adjusters and with the Coast Guard. At night, the others drank beer and watched the rain.

On the third day, the weather dropped. We rode down a coast

still hammered by residual surf. Gulls lofted in a heavy wind. Leaving the track by the river near the lodge, we dropped down onto the long, straight, empty shore. Ahead, a black bear scrambled out of sight. The men strung out single file, riding the surf line on their ATVs. When we reached a place where the river carved a new channel through the sand, they stood up on the footrests to work their way quickly through the current without sinking in. The earth seemed remade in real time, a microcosm of the changes of deep time, the rivers shifting, seas shuffling coastlines, nothing a constant.

New flotsam rimmed the shore, timbers from Japan, Chinese fishing gear, and ribbons of drift net. We saw a great black float that Andy claimed. He'd use it as a lift bag, he said. Other hard, plastic buoys we gathered and dragged to fill the wreck for added buoyancy.

When we reached the boats, we stopped, astonished. The shore was all but unrecognizable. The wrecks were there but dragged far down the beach, surrounded by grounded ice. The rope line to the deadman we'd dug in still held, the only mooring left, but it sang, taut as a fiddle string, the line stretched to a fraction of its original diameter.

"That's a shooter," one said. It carried so much tension it could cut a man apart as it recoiled.

"I think I can get it," Andy said. He bound his knife to a stick. Reached out to slice the straining line. It flew backward, its released spring carrying it almost out of sight back to the sand.

"Guess we dig some more," he nodded at me.

I got a shovel. Steve found scraps of line and doubled them back onto the mooring, making it taut but not dangerously so. We dragged the anchor farther out.

That day, Bill and Ardy tried to get the engines running on the tug. Andy brought out mat jacks, flat cushions that could be slid under the boat and filled with compressed air to raise it. He meant to jack the tug down the beach, using driftwood cribbing as rollers to break the friction with the sand and pulling with an eight-strand block and tackle. The tug lay inland of the barge, just above the surf break at high tide. The barge was lower, and a gut of water nearly reached it already. Andy had contracted with three fishermen in town to run their boats out here to tow the wrecks offshore when they refloated, out the break and back to town.

I gathered stacks of driftwood for cribbing. The men dug under the flat bottom of the tug far enough to place the mat jacks and then filled them with compressed air. The tug rose slowly, inches at a time. Each time, we cribbed it, let the air out of the mats again, and repositioned, until it stood just clear of the sand, breaking the frictional surface.

For want of a better pick point, the men buried empty fifty-gallon drums just above tideline and ran the block to them, rigging it between the drums and the vessel. Eight long strands of line rove between the blocks. Andy braced the near block with a crowbar to keep it from inverting under the strain. When they started the winch, slowly the line pulled forward, one of the men coiling. The boat strained, moving almost imperceptibly. Lurched forward several inches with a jerk. Some of the cribbing fell.

"Let's re-rig."

Again the men dug in the jacks, repositioned the cribbing, and rove out the blocks. Someone saw the sand cracking where the drums were buried. Our pick point was moving. Someone parked one of the ATVs on it for extra weight.

This time the drums began to move as soon as the line came tight. The sand bulged up over them. The pilot jumped on an ATV, jammed its front rack against the tug, and stomped on the gas. Sand flew as the wheels spun out. The tug did not move. Looking at him, the men began to laugh.

"We'll have to re-rig," Andy said, again. But it was too late that day. The incoming tide had walked over the bar. Breakers crashed on the shore again, just below where we were working. We scrambled to unrig the blocks and pack up the jacks, secure our loads onto the ATVs, and cache the tools under a tarp above the high-water line. The air was full of blowing spume. Icebergs spun down the river, and crashed against the choppy, incoming tide. The brief sunlight disappeared in a sudden cloud of fog.

"Let's get out of here."

Single file, we accelerated up the bank to higher ground, crossing the streams and heavy sand, the piles of driftwood in the mist, and dense beach rye. Seagulls lofted off the damp shoreline, where they were picking through debris from the storm. Behind us, the wrecks were hammered by water. There was nothing we could do but wait.

The following morning, we saw a changed world. The barge had moved well down the beach. The tug still sat above the riverline, but the tide had infilled the sand under it again. Again, we dug it out and placed the jacks. The men dragged the barge anchor farther across the tidal flats to hold it from tossing inshore again. I dug a pit to bury the barrels again. This time we lashed them more securely together and buried them deeper, with planks fastened across the front to slow their drag. A winch is only as strong as its pick point.

Foot by foot, the men jacked the tug toward the water once more. By the time we left, they were confident the following day it might refloat, given luck and good weather. The barge, too, lay ready, planks lashed across the hold where one of the hatch covers could not be found. One of its anchors doubled under the barge. The other lay buried out on the tidal flats, holding the barge against the tide.

That night, the fishermen who would tow the vessels to port reached Bering Lake, above the Seal River. They'd wait there overnight and run down to us before the breakers crossed the bar. The men hoped they could hand a towline off and drag the tug off the sand. The barge might be easier, since it lay nearer to the sea. Two of them would ride it out to the bar once it was under tow to keep the pumps going and to dive on the patch if it began to leak. We'd retrieve the anchors in the morning, run the towlines ready, and load tools and gear for the long tow home. Two days perhaps, through open water.

We were on the trail again at dawn. So early the sea smoked with morning mist, calm now, and pearly. A long swell beat on shore, hissing as the sand moved up and down. The air was cold and fresh; it smelled of wet grass, the deep beach rye that can withstand saltwater. Every piece of driftwood cast a small dark shadow as the sun climbed over the mountains. Nothing moved, but there were wolf tracks in the sand. Suddenly we saw them, two gray shapes loping swiftly up into the grass, silvery and wet with dew. One paused, looking back before abruptly vanishing.

When we reached the wrecks, we were all tense, exhilarated with the cold and anticipation. The sun climbed higher, burning off the fog; the day seemed perfect for the work, the clean water and ocean breeze. It would be hot by noon, as hot as it ever got there.

The men rigged the towline to the tug and readied it to pass to the fishing boats. By the time the tide turned, we were standing by. But the boats did not come. The tide crept higher, touched the waterline. Slowly, the tug began to rock, half-floating now, grounding against the shore as the water lifted her, set her back. Still the fishing boats did not appear. We stared upriver. We knew they'd reached the lake last night. Any moment, we thought, we'd see them come.

The men glanced at their watches. The first faint tremors of the swell walked over the bar. The waves roughened, stacking up on the flood, as the river current flowing at eight knots pressed into the oncoming tide. The tide still rose, the tug pounding in surf now, and the fog abruptly reappeared, rising off the water as the sun gained heat. It billowed over the river, blotting out distances into gray mist. In that moment, we saw the other boats.

They came downriver, sailing proudly. Three of them, a pennant on the first. It pulled in toward us, lying just outside the break, and the skipper shouted to our men over the sound of the surf. Andy ran to throw him the end of the towline, already rigged and waiting in his hands. But the boats could no longer pull in close enough. The breaking surf rose too high. The line fell short and was tossed back onto shore. Andy grabbed it and tried again, standing at the very edge of land, where the surf and current churned away the sand. If he fell in, I knew, he might not get out. I moved closer. He tried, and failed again.

"You should go back," he said to me.

I shook my head. No.

"It's better for two people to die?"

I nodded. We both knew I couldn't hold him if he fell. He was too heavy and the current too quick, but I meant to try. I did not want him to stand there alone. He was my friend.

I half expected him to order me back. But he shrugged, half-smiling when he turned back to the sea.

The boat moved farther offshore. The skipper of the first drove at the bank, up-current from the tug, emerging from the fog suddenly bow down on the front side of a breaker. Andy threw the line;

the skipper grappled for it and missed. The breaker ground the boat against the shore. It blew water and sand as the skipper full-throttled backward, trying to escape. For the slightest moment, the boat stuck fast before reversing.

Andy grabbed the line and ran upriver. Just upstream from the tug, the current cut hard against the bluff. The tide had left only a narrow path between the cutbank and the surf; a path already slipping away. He ran past it, out of sight, still trying. And in another moment ran back. He'd thrown the line again, but they could not get it. It swept downriver tied to a buoy, tossing in the break. He handed off the line and ran to rig a fishing pole, a last-ditch attempt to cast a traveling line over the surf while the skipper groped for it.

Once he caught the hook, but the line broke when he tried to pull it in. The shoreline was crumbling. Finally, Andy stopped, defeated.

"We can't get this." He called us away. We ran for it before the tide.

"Tomorrow," he said once we reached high ground. The men began talking, arguing again. Andy's arms waved as he spoke; drawing diagrams in thin air.

Next day, when we returned to the shore, the tug had washed back up the beach again. Again, the men jacked it toward the sea. They told me to dig out the barge anchor. It lay out on the tidal flats, securing the barge from any inward drift, but the sea had buried it so not even the cable was visible now.

I began at the point where the chain sank out of sight, hauling it out of the sand, following its course across the flats. As I moved farther from the boat, the water table rose. Soon the chain was buried below the water table in wet sand that sluffed back into the trench. The faster I dug it out and the harder I tried to lift the chain, the more the sand held it. It was back-breaking work, but it had to be done.

In the distance, the men moved toward the barge, having jacked the tug as far downslope as they could. They loaded cargo from the shoreline onto the deck. I saw them fasten the hatches again and pump off. But I had no time to watch. I worked flat out, digging on hands and knees, soaked through, hair plastered to my face. The chain seemed to go on forever.

When at last I saw the anchor shank, I dug along it, but it was buried so far I could not get a purchase on the flukes. The water kept swallowing it down. Then, at last, I saw Andy coming toward me. He, too, dug as quickly as he could. He got a line around the anchor shank and levered it backward so the flukes released. We dragged it free and loaded it on an ATV to bring to the barge.

When I reached the deck, I saw gear and tools secured in stacks. Mark and Ardy were donning survival gear to ride the barge out. The others were doing a few last tasks, coiling lines, preparing for sea. It was none too soon. The tide was rising. Soon, the water reached the tug again, but this time, the fishing boats were standing by. The men handed off the towline before the breakers crossed the bar.

After so long a struggle, the refloating happened so quickly. A backward haul. The tug and then the barge were gone. We ran up the bank to watch as the tug passed out of sight, the barge behind it, spinning through clouds of fog and sunshine on the water, straight out the bar, and westward on smooth, blue water toward Cordova. Their flags still flying.

"So that's that," someone said.

We waited, resting in deep grass. It was the strangest moment, half sad, half joyful. The boats had come to life again, and all our effort was over.

At last we stirred, walked down the bank, loaded our gear, and rode home. I was fiercely weary, and yet until then I'd felt no pain.

The men pulled out Scotch and shared it back and forth, too tired even to talk that much.

That night we heard over the radio the tug and barge had reached Okalee Spit in safety. They'd anchored there overnight, but all was well. In the morning, we gathered up loose ends to go. It was so quiet now, only the wind and surf, and memories. Soon the grass would wave over our tracks, and all these stories would be from long ago.

Summer of Light and Ice

◆

2011–2012

My first time in Antarctica, I worked in a field camp, WAIS Divide, on the western Antarctic ice sheet. It was an ice core drilling camp, far inland, where the ice sheet was more than two miles thick. The ice divided there, flowing east and west to opposing watersheds in the Ross and Weddell Seas. We were 1,000 miles from the nearest permanent structures at McMurdo, 650 from the South Pole. We figured that summer our closest neighbors were on the space station.

The field season began in late November. Before the scientists arrived, thirteen of us crew flew out from McMurdo on a Hercules equipped with skis to land on the ice. We camped at first in two tiny shelters, like small trailers. Later, we rigged tents for sleeping. Arctic Ovens, blossoming orange as poppies on the snow, were set out in irregular lines with ropes strung between them to serve as guides if a blizzard came.

The tents were unheated. At night, I changed in the communal washroom and ran through the snow to my tent. I had three sleeping bags, each slipped inside the other. I wore two sets of warm clothes to bed. And even so, I often woke scrunched deep at the bottom of the innermost bag, half-suffocated, as cold as ice. Snow tracked in never melted, and water froze, even in thermoses. To shelter our tents, we built walls by cutting the hard, light snow into blocks with knives and stacking the blocks like stones. But some mornings, the wind buried our tent doors in hard-packed snow all the same, and we had to tunnel out. So far out on the ice cap, the wind had a thousand miles of fetch in any direction. It piled the snow in lovely sculptures, hollowing curves here, making mountains there; and the next day, without any apparent change, altering its patterns to gouge a path to someone else's tent.

The wind was our companion, the sky our topography. It was brilliant blue. The ice blue-white under a sun that never set but only inscribed the smallest circle on the sky. Sometimes we felt crushed by the light, as if under a microscope. Sometimes we played tag at midnight. On New Year's Eve we blocked the sun out with cardboard in the windows of the communal Jamesway shelter and pretended it had grown dark at last. It was exhausting, unnerving, to see so much light, even to those of us who'd grown up in Arctic summers.

Sundogs spread out across the sky in concentric jewels. An eclipse temporarily blotted out the sun. Each time the wind rose, blowing snow seemed to fill the air with diamonds. And once that summer we saw a bird, an Antarctic tern lost and far from the sea; the whole camp ran outside to watch it. We were so happy to see something living besides ourselves.

But what I remember most about that austral summer is the way my memories came unmoored. I could no longer say what was true and what was not, where something had happened, or when. I could have been on any continent, or none. Reading in the tent at night, a description of a Russian summer, I could smell the grass and heat of summer, the sourness of a broken jar of pickled mushrooms, as if the page was scratch-and-sniff. I could hear the voices of strangers talking in a room. But when I closed the book, there was only the sound of wind.

I had little time to listen, though. I was low-level staff that austral summer, a brutish job at times, with unreal time pressures and inadequate infrastructure. I moved through those months in a kind of dream, always moving, always half a step ahead of myself in my mind, keeping it together as long as no one spoke to me. It seemed the clock was always counting down, and some days I hardly seemed to see the sky.

But I remember the night they stopped the drill at last, after three seasons boring down through sixty-eight thousand years of solid ice. We drank champagne out of glasses chipped from borehole ice, a little dazed, almost hysterical, mostly happy.

"It was like a knife fight in a phone booth," the chief scientist said, of deciding when to stop the rig. Careers hung on the decision. Because, although the center of the ice sheet was -40°F, as they drilled deeper, the temperature of the ice rose until they came to believe there must be a layer of ground water at its base, formed by sheer pressure. Such water would have been isolated from the biosphere for perhaps a hundred thousand years, and they had no permits to penetrate it. In the end, the chief scientist forced a stop fifty meters above the contact between ice and rock. But I could see the fault lines even yet among the crew, between those who'd wanted to stop, and those who wanted to keep drilling.

They were done now, though in another year they might begin directional drilling. Now, there were only the cores to pack and ship, and the never-ending wind-blown snow to shovel out, keeping access clear to the dome where they had drilled.

Next day, they showed us cores they'd taken. Long, thin, blue-green tubes of crystal ice, they would be sent back to the National Ice Core Laboratory in the United States to be analyzed for bubbles of gases trapped in the ice, dissolved chemicals, and particulate matter. Here, in the stable, deep cold of the ice cap, layers could be seen where each year the snow laid down fresh ice. For thirty thousand years, the annual layers were clear. Earlier seasons could be seen, too, though the weight of ice had deformed them into lower resolution.

One section showed volcanic ash blackening the ice.

"The eruption must have happened very near here," one of the scientists told me. The ash had covered the snow completely for that season. These cores showed also the eruption at Krakatoa, the rise and fall of the Roman Empire, and the dawn of the Industrial Revolution. They showed that concentrations of greenhouse gases were higher now than they had been since the ice sheet first began to form, and that global climates could change in less than ten years, and not return to earlier models. This ice was new when strange beasts walked the earth, at the time of the Pleistocene, before so many extinctions. Sixty-eight thousand years of blowing snow. And yet, in geologic time, it was a blink of an eye. I walked back out of the dome into the relentless light, and it was all so long ago and far away, yet unforgotten, that deep time. I'd spent a season at the edge of so much that I did not understand.

Long ago, before the ice sheet formed, Antarctica was a link between South America and Australia. It shared the paleoclimate of those ancient landmasses, before the continents tore apart, and Antarctica became a still, green, isolated Eden. Species persisted here long after they died out elsewhere. Others arose that never existed elsewhere, giant penguins. Cycads. Blossoming trees.

Then the sea froze as the world cooled. Unhampered by any land mass, the Antarctic Bottom Current swept round the Southern Ocean, farther chilling and isolating it. The ice must have built millimeter by millimeter at times to create this miles-deep sheet that lay in a solid white crust over the pole. The seas now broke against ice cliffs, as the ice cap formed; high mountains, perpetually locked in snow. In places, volcanoes tore the rock; in others, the rock was crushed, metamorphosed into granitic forms. But here and there, sedimentary rocks still preserved the traces of that former, greener world, where glaciers now overhung bright seas glazed with ice.

Antarctica remained a world apart, still sheltered by its isolation. It is colder than the Arctic in part because it is a land mass and less susceptible to the warming influence of the sea. It is also drier, because of the cold. For the most part, its glaciers were now shrinking, driven by the heat. Strangely, though, a few had begun to advance. One night, one of the glaciologists, Sridhar, gave a talk in the galley tent, using a bowl of pudding to explain how glaciers can accelerate for a time because of climate change.

As he scooped more and more pudding into the bowl, it began to run out over the edges. He scraped up the spilled pudding, and piled it back onto the mound, where it promptly overflowed again. It was chocolate.

"I should have used vanilla," he said. "Better visual." As the pudding flowed faster and faster from the bowl, driven by his spoon ferrying scoops to the top, he explained that some Antarctic glaciers work the same way as the bowl of pudding. Because warmer air can hold more moisture, as temperatures rise, precipitation often increases. Here in Antarctica, this warm, damp air is carried inland from the coast and chills as it passes over the ice cap, where it falls in the form of snow. That snowfall in turn compacts into glacier ice, accelerating the glacier's forward march, as it is driven down toward the sea by its own weight. At the sea edge, meanwhile, the face of the glacier keeps melting and breaking off, as the pudding spills over the rim of the bowl. It reenters the atmosphere as moisture, and the process begins again. The glacier's speed can also be accelerated if warming seawater penetrates beneath the glacier face, reducing friction and accelerating melt. For a time, a glacier may retain a balancing point where increased snowfall prevents ice loss, or even increases ice mass. But eventually, if temperatures continue to rise, it will reach a point where it begins to disappear, triggering a cascade of consequences. In Antarctica, loss of glacial ice could trigger sea level rise around the world, so much of the world's water is caught up in this ice cap.

Here at WAIS Divide, the first signals of catastrophe could be seen in those bubbles of air trapped in the ice, with their indelible record of change. We sat in cardboard darkness, on moving ice, and listened. Outside, the wind tore at the Jamesway shelter, as if it would blow us away. How many layers of ice core would suffice to tell the story of this place? This world?

Catching Krill at Midnight, Palmer Deep

◆

December 2014

The krill in our bucket were the color of sunrise. They swam vertically, black eyes bulging, thread-thin legs churning the water, antennae lifted, around the smooth sides of the bucket.

In the wet lab, two men with the happy smiles and graying hair of marine biologists, scooped through them looking for pteropods, the frail, winged butterflies of the sea. These they placed in bags to save for experiments later.

"Want to eat a krill with me, Rosemary?" David offered. He handed it to me, and I swallowed. A fragile, marine flicker on the tongue.

Why did I do that? I wondered.

David grinned and swallowed also.

Back out on deck, the sun had sunk lower over the dark blue water of Palmer Deep. Ice cliffs behind it marked the extent of land. We were far from home, working on a research vessel on the Antarctic Peninsula. I was a marine technician, responsible for deploying scientific gear over the side. David and Marc were biologists studying these smallest creatures, plankton.

The Southern Ocean is biologically immensely productive. Such rich waters occur where upwelling currents drive nutrients from the bottom into the near-surface photic zone, where plankton can photosynthesize. In the Southern Ocean, this process is driven by sea ice. As ice freezes, it forces out salt. Sea ice forms brine channels that slowly drain salinity back into the sea. This chilled, salt-dense water sinks, forcing in turn the deeper, fresher water to rise to the surface from the ocean depths. It also drives the Antarctic Bottom Current, a deep-ocean current circling the continent that acts as a conveyor, cooling the warmer regions of the world by directing warm seawater toward the poles.

Crossing the Drake, on our passage to Antarctica, we cast out XPTs, instruments that measured the temperature of the ocean as they fell slowly through the water column. Watching the screen, we saw a colored line trace out their track on a graph, and the jog left marking that lens of cold water. I blew on my hands, trying to stay warm, watching the colors bloom and fade, as over and over the scientists measured out changes to the ocean temperature over space and time, verifying their theories through sheer repetition.

In the Southern Ocean, trophic levels are simplified to their barest form. Top predators like whales and leopard seals feed directly on primary and secondary producers such as zooplankton, where in warmer climates that chain is often complicated by intermediaries. Furthermore, the land is so cold, limiting runoff, that nearshore waters at the foot of glaciers can be biological hotspots, where in the north, turbidity and runoff often work to create near-dead zones there. As sea ice extent dwindles and temperatures rise, these processes may weaken or even fail.

Krill migrate up and down in the water column, rising upward in the night to feed and sinking in daylight to avoid predators. In summer, they feed on phytoplankton, and in winter on algae growing under the sea ice. They spawn in free fall over thousand-foot-deep ocean canyons, the eggs drifting down until they hatch, and the juveniles in turn slowly rising to the ice edge at the surface. Krill aggregate so densely that the water blooms orange with them at times, and the sea wind takes on an oily smell.

At the edge of a krill swarm, whales cluster, their feces red and greasy with krill. Seabirds gather. There are so many krill, they can seem inexhaustible. But krill are vulnerable, as all things are, to changing weather. In years of poor ice coverage, their numbers fall, and the effects of change at this trophic level can cascade upward. Though the magnitude of loss is as yet unknown, it seems probable that without krill and other zooplankton, many of the other life forms in the ocean would disappear. And yet, zooplankton are so small, that to a krill, ocean water feels as viscous as cold oil. Their sensory parameters are wholly different than ours. They communicate with chemical signals to breed and sense prey by "footprints" of turbulence in the dense liquid that is their medium.

Our next cast came up empty, straining only seawater through the meshes of the trawl. Then, near the end of the night, we caught a ctenophore, a comb jelly six inches long that looked like a translucent, hollow rosebud. Among the simplest of earth's creatures, ctenophores feed by capturing microscopic larvae from ocean water as it flows past the thin, cellular sheets of their bodies. Held to the light, this one showed waving, iridescent lines of cilia sifting the water.

"Look at that beauty," David crowed, delighted. He and Marc kept vigil in the lab through each trawl, in a happy mess of seawater and equipment, while I trundled back and forth deploying nets.

The pteropods themselves were almost invisible, small, dark-shelled animals drifting in the seawater, riding the blurry margin between the plant and animal kingdoms. They are among the most vulnerable of zooplankton to ocean acidification. As human-generated carbon dioxide is absorbed by seawater, it lowers the pH of the water and binds to calcium carbonate, reducing its availability to organisms. Since the Industrial Revolution, anthropogenic carbon dioxide has increased ocean acidity by about 30 percent. Pteropods are threatened by ocean acidification, both because increasing acidification means diminished availability of calcium carbonate to build shells and because the altered pH of the ocean erodes already formed adult shells. As small and vulnerable as pteropods are, they can react to accelerating changes in ocean chemistry that ultimately have the power to affect organisms around the globe. The dangers they suffer could touch us all one day.

But the men liked them for themselves. They shouted each time they found another one.

"You care a lot about them, don't you," I said.

"The heart is a big place," David said.

By dawn we were in sight of the research station, pushing through the brash ice that choked the inlet, up to a pier and a few small buildings clustered on glacial moraine at the foot of the ice sheet. Crabeater seals gathered on the ice, sliding into the sea as we passed, and then, confused by the sound of the ship underwater, leaping back onto the floes again. Like a raft, one floe swung in to touch the ship where its steel side broke the water. The floe crumpled when it struck. The seals tumbled back into the water again, graceful as soon as they touched the sea.

Late morning, we off-loaded the krill into the tiny lab space at the station. I went directly to the boathouse.

Late that night, I went back to the station laboratory and saw David intent on his task. Slowly, he inserted a sensor into one of the krill, to measure if part of its intestines was an anaerobic environment. On the screen before him, a pteropod was magnified to visible size. It swam slowly, extraordinarily gracefully, with those lovely wings too small to see with the naked eye.

He smiled at me as I came in.

"Watch this," he said. "It's beautiful."

Carefully, he moved the sensor forward.

Adélie/Gentoo

◆

January 2015

Five of us hunched in the Zodiac as it pushed through brash ice near the foot of the glacier. Ice cliffs shellacked with glistening snow rose above the black rock of the waterline. Antarctic terns scattered as we passed. Ahead, a set of black-backed penguins dolphined out of the sea in a quick, smooth line.

We passed a shoal where elephant seals lay hauled out, groaning and belching, lurching on top of piles of their neighbors to let their bodies sink down into the heap of seals. They were females, each weighing perhaps two thousand pounds, slick mounds of deep diving blubber. They raised their heads to watch us with beautiful dark eyes. But the stench was something overwhelming.

"They will stick their faces in their own shit and blow bubbles," one of the scientists observed.

I didn't answer. I thought he was being disrespectful. Even though it was true. Besides, I was driving the Zodiac, as a marine technician, not a biologist.

Ahead, we were approaching the penguin rookery. We could smell it, too, before we saw it. The snow was smeared red with penguin feces, greasy with krill. I cut the motor to let us drift in quietly, and a woman climbed out to tie off the boat.

We stepped out onto the rocks and pulled off our immersion suits. We'd reached a small lagoon, penguins gathered along its shore. On the rocks above us, more penguins nested. The air was full of the soft, clear sound of their voices.

The penguins watched us incuriously. Now, late in the austral spring, the chicks waited, absurdly fluffy, with soft bodies and angular wings, for adults to bring them food from the sea. In tide pools at the foot of the rocks, the adult penguins gathered, tumbling in and out of the water. Some were now returning from the sea, making their way out of the water in a smooth bound. Transformed from grace by the medium of air, they waddled through the shallows on all but nonexistent legs, up the shore to the colony. They walked like human children just learning not to fall.

I watched as one penguin fell on its stomach to propel itself forward with wings like oars along a smooth sled track in the snow that had been worn deeper by successive penguins. When it reached its nest, it called to its chick. They nibbled at each other's beaks, and then the parent disgorged its full stomach into the mouth of the waiting chick. The other parent left, as the first settled down.

We were there to recapture a satellite tag left by the birders a few days before. They'd marked the bird carrying the tag with a waterproof cattle marker, for easy identification in a crowd of almost identical penguins. It looked as if they'd crayoned on its paper-white belly in blue and green.

One of the women held the receiver, a small antenna of crossed wires.

"It's here," she said.

The others fanned out along the shore, looking at birds just returning from the sea. I stood to the side, watching the colony. A skua drifted overhead, waiting to catch a chick. Offshore, I could see the detritus of a leopard seal's feeding awash in the shallows, the back and wings of a penguin jerked inside out, skinned and swallowed. It floated like a rag, wings spread, head down.

Penguin bones lay beside my feet. I picked up a wing, a broad blade of bone like an enlarged scapula, then laid it back as it had been. In life, it would be covered with skin and fine feathers almost like hide. Penguins are flightless, but they use their wings in swimming. Their bodies are smooth and unbelievably sturdy, their skulls hard bone. But their eggs are as lovely as flowers, soft blue or palest orange inside a shell of changeable gray.

At the water's edge, one of the birders began to move rapidly. He'd seen the penguin. Three of them converged on it with a small dipnet, catching it on the first try and holding it still to remove the satellite tag. It fought hard. One of the women gripped its wings to subdue it, holding them to its body so it could not club her and holding its strong feet. It stabbed at her with an almost reptilian bite.

The others removed the tag quickly. They'd download the data back in camp and later replace the tag on another penguin, supergluing it into place for a few days. The satellite transmitters gave information about dive depth and frequency and would hopefully provide insight into forage behavior.

As sturdy as these birds were, the colony was in jeopardy. The Antarctic Peninsula is the fastest warming place on earth. Adélie penguins in particular are hardwired to nest at certain times, and if they are unable to do so because of heavy snow or meltwater flooding the nest site, they will not breed until the following year. This close link to a particular place and climate is why they have thrived in such a harsh environment, but with it comes loss of flexibility, and now those very ties may doom them. Even if they are able to nest, the increased moisture and higher winds in the changing climate of the Antarctic Peninsula seem to drastically reduce chick survival. They die of hypothermia, and they also die if their parents can't find food.

But current flows structure local ecology and may be changing. If the sea ice retreats too far from land, birds like these that forage along the ice edge could be in trouble. Later, I worked for a time with scientists who modeled ocean currents in space and time, using gliders and conductivity-temperature-depth measurements; acoustic surveys of krill distribution; and penguin foraging behavior to demonstrate how current flows structure the local ecology, including how krill distribution may be changing with changing climate patterns.

Through the season, I watched as scientists deployed and recovered the bright yellow underwater gliders that carried their instruments. They worked to determine how far from shore the krill were gathering and how far the penguins had to swim to find a meal.

Some nights the birder group did lavage as part of their forage study, catching penguins returning from the sea and inducing them to regurgitate part of their catch before they reached their nests. The birders were uncomfortable with the work. Sometimes, they told me, the bird died, and in any case its chick could miss a meal, its survival margin already razor-thin. But it seemed necessary to do this thing, to understand the problems facing the colony as a whole, and so they did it, gathering data that could be got no other way.

Mornings after the lavage nights, the birders sat at a lab table under bright lights, sifting through the penguins' stomach contents with tweezers. If the bird had caught its prey close to shore, the krill were still whole, smooth pink bodies in the petri dish, looking edible even to me. But if the bird had had a long swim from deep water, the krill would have begun to digest already. Then the stomachs would be filled with a smellier, greenish mash of bodies disintegrating into slime. Despite the temporary abundance, it seemed that overall, birds were having to travel farther from the colony to seek their meals, as their nesting success also waned. It was possible that in our lifetimes, there would no longer be Adélies at the station, something once impossible to imagine.

But I remember one morning, early, before the rest of camp was stirring, I went outside in blowing snow to check the boats. On the pier, I saw a single penguin. As I stood there watching, in the still-dark of predawn and the heavy snow, it walked toward me carefully on small pink feet.

"Quarrk?" it said, a liquid question.

I cleared my throat. "Quarrk," I said, hoping it would respond.

It walked up quietly to stand beside me. Almost as if we were friends. As if we could be. Or as if I shared some knowledge of its fate.

Leopard Seals

◆

Austral Summer, 2014–2015

We headed for Humble Island, myself and five birders in a skiff. I worked in the boathouse then, at a research station on the western Antarctic Peninsula. They were checking petrel nests; I drove. We worked our way through brash ice left by the calving glacier. The water here had only recently been exposed by its retreat.

Crossing, we saw splashing at the edge of the ice and the long, dark head of a leopard seal. It was feeding. The body of a crabeater seal bobbed in the water, a long blood smear marking the surface. The leopard seal eyed and took another bite, working its way around the crabeater as if it were eating an ear of corn. The crabeater spun in the water.

We cut the motor and drifted, watching the seals. The one still feeding, the other now unrecognizable, a mass of flesh. There was a wreck near here, where the divers believed leopard seals cached meat; an eerie, dark place, where we often saw them, drifting, waiting. The divers were afraid of the seals, and rightly so. Humans, too, had been killed by leopard seals. And yet, most of the time, the seals showed only curiosity. It was their lack of fear of us that made us fear them. How hard to understand the lives of animals perpetually harried by our actions as well.

And leopard seals are not simple to understand. They have been documented seemingly trying to share their food with humans, pushing mouthfuls of meat at divers trying to retreat. Even the dead woman might have been killed in play.

Leopard seals are individuals. Some eat seals, some krill. Others steal from each other. It is strange to remember they are filter feeders also, their back teeth specialized for plankton. Perhaps the earliest whales fed this way, macrophage in the front, filtering in the back. We are all such a patchwork of evolutionary false starts, patchworks, holdovers, and not yet fully realized adaptions; each species perfect in the moment, each also in a continual becoming.

Earlier that season, I'd seen leopard seals following us. I heard them singing under the ice in glassy stillness, an eerie, haunting sound that seemed to come from every direction and none. I saw one circle our skiff and dive under it, its long body twisting far below us in transparent water, extraordinarily graceful, immensely fast. It was difficult to separate its curiosity from our fear.

They played with their food, too, as children do. Once we saw one repeatedly attack a young elephant seal, letting it swim a little way, then surging back up out of the depths. In the end the battle drifted out of sight. But later, some of the station staff found an elephant seal pup that was fiercely wounded but still alive. We thought it was the same one, and that the leopard seal let it go. But if it let it go, it had perhaps never intended to kill it at all. It was all a game.

After feeding, leopard seals slept for hours or days, each hauled out solitary on floating ice. Never on land, never together. A nine-foot tube of shining muscle slumped across the cracks and hummocks of the ice drifting slowly past glacial shores.

I once woke to find one on the floating dock, halting our work-day until it chose to go. I went down the dock with one of the bird-ers. He touched it very lightly with a long pole. For the barest sec-ond I caught my breath. Then it reacted with inconceivable rapidity, lunging at us, from deep sleep to full awareness in a heartbeat, as if nothing in life had ever touched it deliberately before. It did not quite make contact. It could have, maybe, but it did not, and after that first astonished lunge, it held back.

For a moment it paused, staring in seeming disbelief. Then it swung away and slid off the floating dock, a length of smooth muscle and bone. Its flippers hung for a moment still on the dock. And then it was gone.

I remember, too, the first time I saw one, when I was new to leopard seals, my first week at the boathouse. A Zodiac tied at the dock was working loose. I knelt to retie it to the cleats. A leopard seal rose to look at me, our faces truly nearly touching. It was so un-expected, I felt no threat, only a deep curiosity. Its eyes were black, the pupils huge, rimmed with a narrow, pinkish sclera. Its skin shone wet silver from the sea. It looked into my eyes, as I looked in its. For a long moment, time seemed to stop. I held quite still and watched until the seal released me from its unwavering gaze, slid beneath the water, and disappeared. It was in charge of our communication. All I could do was stand at the threshold of its world and wonder, watch-ing the surface shiver where it had been, seeing the terrible glory of the world.

I thought, "I could have kissed it." It was so close.

And, for a long moment, I wished I had.

Wilhelmina Bay

◆

May–June, 2017

Dawn on the ship, heavy snow. I shoveled the Zodiacs before the light came up and readied them for launching from the deck. In the distance, whales surfaced along the ice edge. Others rolled and breathed off our stern.

When the researchers were ready, we launched the boat, lifting it on the crane hook over the side. I swung into it over the rail, and the bosun lowered me with it on the crane to the ocean surface. Unhooked, I pulled forward to get the others at the Jacob's ladder.

These researchers were tagging whales and taking biopsies here on the western Antarctic Peninsula. I would take the photos for picture ID and drive the boat. The men, checking their gear, were tense. Over the last few days, they'd already deployed ten tags on feeding whales. Today we were seeking only biopsies, using a plug fired from a crossbow that collected a small tissue sample.

In the austral fall, krill aggregate at the heads of bays where sea ice first begins to form. Humpback whales follow them there to feed before migrating north to breed. As we neared the ice edge, I saw whales thicker than I had ever seen. It seemed as if I could have walked on water, stepping from whale to whale across their backs.

By then it was snowing so hard the snow built up on the surface of the water in a gray sheen broken by the flukes and backs of whales, who were feeding in clusters so tight they all but brushed against each other. But each whale knew where the others were. They knew where we were, too, moving slowly and as quietly as we could. Some did not react. Others slapped their flukes in mild anger. Those we left alone.

At the edge of the brash ice, we singled out a whale and followed it; one crew member was at the tiller while another crouched in the bow giving directions under his breath. The whale moved slowly through loose ice, letting us near. We idled in as closely as we could without disturbing it.

I was so cold, my fingers almost would not bend. But I gripped the camera. The scientists waited until I had a clear photograph of a whale's flukes so that it could be identified later, then watched for the first signs of humpbacks rising underwater. Only once a photo had been taken would they fire a biopsy dart.

As we waited for one to fluke, we watched their dorsals to tell them apart. Even there, I was surprised how easily I could identify individual whales. Their flukes and dorsals were as individual as faces.

Once a whale was photographed, we moved closer, guessing from turbulence—called footprints—from its flukes, where the whale would turn and surface near enough for the men to reach. As it broke the water, its smooth black back close beside our Zodiac, one of the men knelt on the bow and shot with the crossbow, barely nicking the whale. It submerged and drenched us with spray.

"Got it," he said.

The arrow floated to the surface, the neon capsule at its end containing a tiny tissue plug from the whale. It would be analyzed for contaminant loads, stress hormones, diet, and genetic information. It could also show the gender and pregnancy status of whales in the area, helping to build baseline data that could be used to establish protections for them.

Other whales surfaced in the distance, their high spouts drifting mist across the glacier face. We followed, seeking further samples.

That evening, when it came time to go back to the ship, we had been drifting in neutral for some time, observing. I put the Zodiac in gear and turned. At that moment, a whale surfaced beside us, so close it all but hit our boat. If it had, it would have spilled us in the freezing water. I realized it had known where we were and trusted us to stay there. When we began to move, we'd crossed its path and nearly lost the boat.

Next morning dawned pearly clear, the snowstorm gone. We launched early and soon were running far out on the bay. We saw a whale moving in drifting ice. Lost it. Could not see another, and so began to work our way down through the bay. Our last day of sampling, and suddenly the whales were gone. Who knew why? Sometimes they simply vanished, and we were left holding our empty wishes to the impenetrable, unspeaking sea.

The glacier rumbled, calving ice into the sea. The surface of the water began to smoke as the sun struck it. Day had begun. Far off we could see the orange sides of the research vessel. We were running west now along the shore. Watching brash ice. Watching. It could move against the wind on unseen currents, surrounding you almost before you could believe it.

Near the entrance to Wilhelmina Bay, we saw a mother and calf, almost too close under the glacier face to reach. We photographed them and then lost sight of them. Drifting, as we waited for the lost whales, we watched the surface of the water.

Then we heard singing. A whale floated under us, a shadow directly beneath the boat. It was singing. Singing to us perhaps? Suddenly, the men burst into gale of laughter at seeing the whale so near. Laughter at the excitement, at a job well done, cold and exhilaration, so far from home.

Moving again, the throttle cable came loose. I crouched to hold it into place, still driving, too happy to go back to the ship, surrounded by whales once again.

At one time humpbacks were all but hunted out of Antarctic waters and butchered by hundreds of thousands in whaling stations on the sub-Antarctic islands. When whale hunting was banned in the Southern Ocean in 1985, humpback populations began to recover. Though now the commercial harvest of krill and changing ocean conditions may threaten those gains. That was the underlying question many of these scientists sought to answer. What happens next? What can we do to mitigate disaster?

Though the population is now recovering, no one knows how many whales were once here. Some scientists believe that despite the numbers we were seeing, there were once perhaps ten times as many humpbacks. Some even think that, though humpback whales feed on krill, they actually support enhanced krill populations by their presence. The reason is that whale feces, rich in surface nutrients, sink through the water column, fertilizing at all levels. The presence of whales, like the presence of many predators, may drive vitality through the entire ecosystem. It's possible we have never seen what a truly functional ecosystem can be like; our imagination, like our understanding, may be simply impoverished.

In the austral summer of that year, these men and their team worked from a research station on shore. There, I ran the boathouse, before we transitioned to the ship. The whales were thick around station that year, feeding in pairs, mothers and calves, or unrelated adult whales, perhaps for companionship or help in surrounding prey. They were bubble-feeding, blowing bubbles deep underwater around schools of krill to spook them into a tighter swarm, and then rising, wide mouthed, through the clustered krill to gulp them up.

Looking down from the Zodiac, I saw the pale, clear bubbles hissing on the surface as they broke and then the swift, enormous movement of the whale as it surfaced open-mouthed beside the boat. Breaking the surface, it all but struck us, rolling on its side as it did so, the tight lips of its blowhole smacking open. Its rough skin was smeared with white scars, tiny bites from cookie-cutter sharks, and barnacles. I saw its eye, deep in wrinkled skin, and the great pleated mass of its throat.

Meanwhile, these researchers prepared their work, intent even in the thrill of the moment. They cared about the whale at a deep level, about its life apart from them, its independent concerns, and its brief interaction with our boat.

Each year at high summer the whales return from their breeding grounds in west Australia or north along the coast of South America. They feed through summer, into fall, then fast during their long trek north. Data from this research had already shown the importance of certain areas, such as Wilhelmina Bay, to their year-round lives. There are few places where they can feed enough to last throughout the breeding season as they do here. These key places, and the fall ice edge, are a great part of the reason that there are whales in South America and Australia.

It is not known for certain how humpbacks find their prey, but researchers believe that mothers teach their young to return to the same places every year, navigating the vast stretches of the sea on a scale of time and place unknowable to us. Back across the starry reaches of the ocean, to this small place, Wilhelmina Bay, without which there might be so many fewer whales.

Southern humpbacks are not known to cross the equator and mingle with their northern brethren, but behavioral traits such as bubble-feeding may have spread through cultural transmission down from the far north. Their wintering calving grounds are not far apart. There may be gene flow from this place throughout the world, and through deep time. These whales are named for their great flippers; their Latin family name, *megaoptera*, translates as "mighty wing." They are the most graceful, almost balletic of the baleen whales; they are known to sing, and to learn songs from each other. Sometimes they will hurl themselves out of the water, breaching for no known reasons, in what looks to an observer like joy.

In the north, I knew them from my childhood, growing up on boats in Southeast Alaska. There they are at risk from cruise ship traffic, commercial fishing gear, and naval exercises. Of all whales, and all creatures, it is the humpback whales that wring my heart. They are so perfectly what they are, so much a part of time and place. In Southeast summers or Southern winters, the ocean comes alive through the body of a humpback, flinging itself out of the water or cruising rockbound shores. Singing.

Once, years ago, I saw one breaching near Naked Island in Prince William Sound. I was commercial fishing alone, on a small boat, the *Solitaire*. That summer I was always nearly out of money, always half-broken down. And yet, that summer day when I saw the whale, I killed the motor and for an hour just drifted with the summer wind, the cool, bright air, the blues and greens of summer on the sea as the whale danced and sang below my boat. Of all the days that summer, that is the one that mattered most. It was worth more than all the fish I never caught.

Perhaps it is living still. Perhaps right now the whales are feeding somewhere in the Southern Ocean, shoulder to shoulder, diving deep. Perhaps that magic is still real.

Guillemot of Cooper Island

◆

Summer 2016

Late August is no longer summer in the Arctic. Holding a notebook and pencil in one hand, shotgun in the other, I stamped my feet to stir warmth in my body as I watched Penelope carefully lift a half-fledged guillemot chick from the nest.

It squeaked and fought her.

"Hey, buddy, I know," she said. With practiced hands, she stilled its wings and slid it into a small cloth bag attached to a scale. A tall, thin, quiet girl with reddish hair, Penelope had spent years weighing guillemots.

"240 grams," she said.

I marked it in the column in my notebook. Tipping the bird gently from the bag again, she spread its wing against a ruler.

"135 millimeters. This guy could fledge."

Earlier, she'd marked its leg with a small blue band that identified it as a bird from Cooper Island. If it fledged and survived its first winter, as only a handful of fledglings do, and if it came again to the island another year, the birders would know it was from here.

"Three sculpins in the nest," Penelope added.

Released, the bird shook itself and scuttled back into the nest box. Penelope and I moved to the next nest, trudging over wind-worn sand at the edge of the Beaufort Sea.

We were working on a seabird study banding black guillemots on Cooper Island, east of Utqiaġvik, Alaska. Small alcids with a swift, erratic flight, boldly patterned in black and white, black guillemot winter along the ice edge and nest in summer on the Arctic coast. They are cavity nesters, so normally they would not have been found on barrier islands, but Cooper Island supported a small colony, the only one of its kind along this coast.

The biologist whose project this was, George Divoky, came to Cooper Island forty years before; he was a young man then. He'd stumbled upon guillemot nesting here in packing crates abandoned by the military, in a place where they were not said to nest at all. In subsequent summers he returned to the island, building more nest sites for the birds and documenting their numbers, chick weights, fledge timing, and nest success. For forty seasons, he'd watched that small initial population expand to a high of two hundred breeding pairs during his first summers on Cooper Island. Watched as they hatched, and fledged, and returned. Watched as the climate changed in his own lifetime. That early abundance gave way to a precipitous drop in nest success, when the sea ice edge moved farther from the shore in summer.

According to him, that drop was caused by changes in prey abundance due to warming Arctic waters. Guillemots feed largely on Arctic cod, which are dependent on sea ice cover at certain stages of their lives. Divoky believed that guillemots followed the cod, feeding farther off shore, which limited the number of times they could carry food to their chicks each day. Chicks fledged with lower body weights, lessening their chances of survival. Others died of starvation in the nest. There were now scarcely half the breeding pairs that had been on Cooper Island a decade or two before.

At the same time, polar bears began to appear on the island in summer. Isolated by disappearing sea ice, they preyed on the guillemot eggs and chicks. In response, Divoky invested in a series of bear-proof nest boxes that now lay scattered across the island like a windfall of small black suitcases. Each box was numbered; many contained nesting birds. He knew the location and history of each nesting pair; indeed, he knew the location and history of each piece of driftwood on the island, each bone, sometimes I thought each blade of grass.

Divoky's work became an account of forty years of nest success in the boxes he had built, with fledge dates and fledgling weights. He'd transmuted this record of a human-made colony into a tale of ice-obligate species and climate change. That central story of unimaginably rapid warming and of shifts in weather patterns driving change at a scale we could not fathom was inarguable, palpable, immediate, and real to anyone with experience in the Arctic. Once this had been a place of snow and ice and birds. Now we walked on bare sand, counting the missing. And he had been there as it happened.

Divoky had left the island for the season. Penelope and I were waiting for the last chicks to fledge before we, too, would go. Last week for two days the parent birds had stopped bringing in food. Watching the chicks' weights slide, we compiled a list of chicks we thought would surely die. But somehow, they'd beaten the odds. Next morning when we walked our rounds, the nest boxes were full of sculpin, and only one nestling had died. We found his body beside a pile of fish. They'd come too late; he'd been too weak to swallow them.

The other chicks had grown from gray, fluffy balls into pale adolescents, their smooth white wings flecked with sooty gray. They crouched on mucky sand in the bottom of the nest boxes. Guillemots try to shit outside the nest, but some chicks had better aim than others. A few fish lay at the entrance to some nests. Guillemots size the fish they bring to the nest to the size of the chick that will swallow it, and these sculpin were large, for fledging birds.

"Tomorrow," Penelope said. "I bet tomorrow we see a lot of empty boxes." The birds would have flown away.

Back at the camp we tried to dry out and get warm. Divoky had a small cabin for cooking and a sleeping tent, but neither could be heated. We were often damp through from the raw sea fog.

That afternoon, we set out noose mats, trying to snare birds carrying temperature-depth transmitters that Divoky had put on the week before he left. It was our job to recapture them lest they stay on all winter. We'd gotten back all but two, but those birds seemed no longer to be returning to the nest. The chick in nest P3 had died, so the transmitter on that parent bird was lost. But there was still some chance we might get C1.

We buried a mat in front of its nest box, carefully pulling out and arranging the nooses made of heavy fishing line into an all-but-invisible circle of snares. I stood, waiting by the camp and keeping my eyes on the box. An hour passed, and another. There were many birds in the pond that day, bobbing with fish gripped in their beaks. They watched us and darted to the nest boxes when our backs were turned. They knew where we were looking, and they were afraid of us.

At last, I saw a flutter of black-and-white wings, flapping up and jerking back to the earth, tied like a child's balloon to the nest box where we'd set the snares. I ran to it, calling Penelope. She was close behind me, her heavy birder's vest weighted with books, pencils, bands, and tools. I caught the bird and held it to keep it from injuring itself, folding its wings in to its body. She took it from me and tried to free it from the noose. The fishing line had bitten into the skin of its foot, and it took a moment to work it loose.

"It's the wrong bird," she said.

There was no transmitter. We'd caught the mate, the third time in a row that had happened. Upset to have disturbed it to no purpose, Penelope bit her lip, held it up, and tossed it lightly into the sky. It fell slightly before gaining momentum and sped away from us to open ocean in a blur of wings.

"How many times have we caught that bird?" she asked.

I told her, but she already knew. She bit her lip again.

"Let's pull the mat," she said at last. "We can try again tomorrow. I think we've harassed this bird enough for now."

"I think the mate might be dead," she added. "It's been a while since we've seen it."

We walked back to the cabin slowly, catching our breath. It was hard to run on the soft sand. Already, the sun dipped toward evening. We kept early hours on the island.

Next morning, sea fog had settled over camp. It drifted in dense, cold breaths across the island, obscuring everything more than a few yards from the cabin. We waited indoors hoping it would lift. When the sky began to clear, I stepped outside.

"Uh oh," I said.

A white shape appeared in disappearing fog. Just beyond the bear fence, in the nearest part of the colony, a polar bear nosed at one of the nest boxes. It picked it up and flipped it with a soft, heavy paw. I reached inside the door and grabbed a gun. Penelope followed. We stood together on the threshold, watching the bear.

"He looks so tired," Penelope whispered. "Doesn't he look like a tired old man?"

"He's so big," I said.

Its belly seemed to drag between its legs. Back at the Arctic Research Facility, in Utqiaġvik, they had a chart called the Polar Bear Fatness Index. It showed pictures of bears on a continuum from emaciated to obese, for the purposes of data recording. This one was massive.

It lifted the box again with its teeth, holding it by the handle, set it down, and fumbled with the latch.

"If you skin them, their paws are almost like hands," a hunter back in Utqiaġvik had told me. "It's amazing what they can do."

And one of the biologists told stories of Irish, a bear that many years ago had been kept in captivity in Utqiaġvik by the Naval Arctic Research Laboratory. "I gave him a mouse once, and he gutted it. He left all the entrails perfectly arranged. You wouldn't have believed that you could do that with claws like that. And then he just stood there looking at me."

"Looking at you like, 'You're next?'" I asked.

"Maybe," he said. "I don't know. Just . . . looking at me."

Giving up on the latch, the bear stepped onto the box with both its front paws and let its weight fall sharply down, repeatedly trying to crush it as bears will do to break through ice into a ringed seal den. It did not give. The bear turned away, and moved toward the cabin.

"Hello?" Penelope called a warning.

It stopped, half rose, and swung its head trying to see us. Penelope called again. We tightened our grip on our guns.

It dropped to the sand and hustled away, breaking into a run as it passed out of sight over drifted sand between us and the sea. For a moment we could see its back, still running, paralleling the shore. Then the dune grew steeper, and it disappeared.

"I bet he spends the day on the east end," Penelope said. The ground was higher there, and bears seemed to like to sleep there during the day

Later, she and I went out to check on the upended nest boxes. Sand and gravel drifted inside. One chick had been buried in it. She picked it out, tucked it under her thigh, and swiftly patted the gravel back in place.

"I know, little buddy. It's been a rough day," she said.

It tried to bite her, as they all did.

"It's got to be scary, having your home upended like that," I said.

"I saw a bear once fall asleep with its head on one of the nest boxes," she told me. "I had to wonder what the chick inside was thinking."

Midmorning, we saw the bear again, making a day den a mile down the beach to the east. We kept an eye on it throughout the day as we went about our chores, weighing chicks, hauling water, maintaining camp. It stayed asleep, a great white mound, seemingly as fat as two bears.

That evening, on a narrow strip of sand just offshore, we saw another bear. It'd been napping, concealed by driftwood, but it got to its feet when a skiff from the village went by. Smaller than the first, it rested on its haunches, looking around, then settled back to sleep again.

Penelope and I looked at each other.

"Yikes," I said.

In the morning, when we woke, the bears were gone. The following day, with no further sightings, we decided to walk to the east end of the island. We were collecting polar bear hair for a biologist back in Utqiaġvik who used genetic data from the follicles for a mark-recapture study. We wanted to check the day den for scraps of fur, so we set off along the shore, carrying guns, following the broad, shallow tracks of the polar bear. It was a windy day, the sky gray with coming snow.

Penelope and I walked the barren shore, watching for pellets cast by peregrines or other predator birds and for bands from dead guillemots. The bones of whales and seal, weathered whitish gray, protruded from the highest drifts. Cooper Island was once a whaling camp, where people from the mainland came to stay during the hunt. There were shaped timbers also, half buried in sand, from Yankee whalers wrecked near here over a hundred years ago. Blackened sand where hunters made a fire last spring.

The bear had made its day den under a sandy dune and against driftwood to be out of the wind. We found slight impressions in the sand, a scooped out hollow, and many tracks. Tiny, fine white hairs glistened in the grass, tugged at by the Arctic wind. We stripped our gloves off to gather them. Penelope held a manila envelope, while I thrust hairs into it one by one, my fingers clumsy with the cold. It seemed strange to touch them. The bear felt so near, and yet also as if it were something out of the past, already doomed maybe by humans, frightened though we were of it.

On our walk home, we did not talk much. The wind had tugged the feeling out of us. The day been too much. Too big, too bright, it overstretched us.

Soon after that, we left the island. Two scientists from Utqiaġvik came out to help us pack. We built a fire that evening on shore and sat up for a long time, talking, listening. That night all four of us stayed in the tent, sand on the floor, the acrid smell of bird shit in the air. We spent the following day breaking down camp, boarding up the cabin, and loading the skiff.

That last morning, before the long ride home to Utqiaġvik, we made the round of the nest boxes together. Again, not all the chicks had left, though they still seemed to be at fledging size. Penelope speculated that those periods of late-season near-starvation might still be affecting them, even though they seemed to have resumed normal growth patterns. But if the fledglings waited too long, they risked losing their recent weight gains and having less chance of surviving on their own.

"Maybe it's taking them a while to catch back up in other ways," Penelope said.

"You should be gone, little buddy. Go!" she said, carefully setting a bird back at the entrance to its nest box.

We finished the last nests in silence. It seemed so incomplete still, a journey not yet finished. It tugged at our hearts. We'd never know for sure what happened, unless some year, by chance, one of them returned. If peregrines didn't get them. If they learned to fish, if the water stayed open. If these chicks survived through their first year, they could live to be thirty or more. They might raise chicks of their own here on the island. But for now, though, they were just a mark on a column, "Assumed Fledge." And all the rest was still to come.

We turned toward Utqiaġvik and home once more, leaving the island to the wind and fog.

At the Eider Perch

◆

April–May 2015

Eiders moved at the head of the lead, a scribble of dark wings rising and falling.

"Look!" I raised my binoculars to count. Set them down as the birds arrowed past, their wings breaking the glassy stillness of the air in a musical whisper, their sturdy bodies bright against the sky.

Vera marked the number on a sheet of paper. A thousand king eider, more males than females. Sea ducks, the females dark, the males patterned black and white with brilliant orange and blue colors on their crowns.

"Beautiful. Is so beautiful," Vera said, her thin, young face temporarily alight.

She and I had been watching for an hour from a windbreak on shore-fast ice in the Chukchi Sea. The lead had opened up that morning after days of loose ice clogging against the pressure ridge where we sat. Now it lay, a wide, blue crack across the absolute white of the ice to either side. Vera sighed, lit a cigarette, shuffled her feet to keep them warm. I climbed up on the ice behind our perch and scanned the horizon with binoculars. No polar bears, only the glinting, prismatic white of shattered ice.

We were there, she a student sent as part of a research collaboration effort from St. Petersburg, Russia, and I from Fairbanks, to count eider migrating along the Beaufort and Chukchi seacoasts to nesting grounds in the eastern Arctic. So far, though, we had seen few eider. East winds throughout the spring had slowed their migration. Weather patterns were changing fast. There were higher winds and a thinner, shorter-lived ice pack. But sooner or later, we hoped, the birds would come.

I looked back to the water while Vera watched for birds. I heard a breath. We both turned.

Two bowhead whales rose near the head of the lead. We heard their soft exhalations across the water and saw the slow lift of their black backs as they crossed the lead. A mother and calf. They paused just before the perch and hung there breathing, rising slowly and falling, one breath—two—three—before moving on. That morning one had breached, a spectacular explosion from the depths of the sea as the whale rose fully into the air and crashed back. Bowhead whales are among the largest animals on earth and may be the longest lived, their lives fueled by a slow burn of plankton as they drift like dirigibles through the Arctic waters.

"Birds," Vera said. A smaller flock this time, undulating over broken ice. They broke into view already past us. A group of about thirty took the lead, followed by a line of perhaps a hundred more, overtaking each other and falling back. We never got used to the sight, it caught us the same way every time, something lovelier almost than you could believe.

"One hundred and seventy," I said.

"No," Vera said. "Two hundred."

We looked at each other. We tried so hard to get it right. There are wide margins of error on a count like that, and observer bias is inevitable. But in time our numbers came to nearly converge.

To the west of us, Iñupiat whale hunters had made a camp at the edge of the lead. They were out now in their skin boat, waiting for the whales. If they could get within striking distance, they would try first with a light harpoon with a float attached, and then, once that marker was secured, give a killing stroke with a black powder or penthrite bomb. Many times the whale would swim under the ice and get away. It would be counted against the quota all the same, and the loss to the community would be significant.

At the rim of the lead, blocks of ice stood upright, breaking the smooth transition of ice to water. They were set there to break the whale's line of sight and hide the hunters. Sometimes the men stood there for hours, dressed in long white parkas, watching for whales in the lead. If they saw one that looked near enough, they launched their boat, sliding down the ice, and paddled after it.

A young hunter, still flushed and awed with success, told me of standing on the ice edge as a first-year whale swam along it.

"I could see its eyes," he said. "It was looking at me."

It rose steadily below him, watching him, but rising within range of the killing stroke. He darted his harpoon and saw it strike. The whale died at once. Some whalers believe that the whales give themselves, offering their bodies to the hunter in acknowledgment of the bond between the people and the whale. Watching how the whales rested at the surface, breathing softly, the lift of their breath making their bodies rise and fall in the water, still waiting, letting the whalers travel within their reach, it was easy to believe that this was so.

As yet, there'd been no strike in this camp. Whaling is an arduous way to live, requiring days spent waiting in the cold; sleepless nights watching the water during the brief window in spring when the whales passed. If the pack ice swung in and crushed the shore-fast ice in the explosion of force called *ivu*, if the ice broke off and drifted away, or if a pressure ridge collapsed, the camp could be obliterated. Yet this was their way, who they were. A whole community was supporting these hunters here on the ice.

At the trail leading to the eider perch, two canvas tents stood: our warm-up tent and that of a whaling crew. The men were asleep in there now, having whaled all night when the wind came down. As I watched, a head poked out of the door. An older man looked around and slowly climbed out.

He called out softly as he climbed the perch. Sound carries under ice, and whales have good hearing. Lit a cigarette. He put a compass on the perch desk as he came in.

"You should always keep a compass," he said. "If it turns, the ice is moving."

Vera poured him coffee. I dug out our bag of candy to share. He reached down and turned up our VHF so he could hear the talk of hunters along the coast.

All of the ten or so camps out there had a VHF, and all stood by on the whaling channel, separate from the one used in the town. They talked about the ice, bears seen, and whales passing; it was a quiet, intermittent read on circumstances along the coast. It was sometimes difficult for us to understand what the hunters said because we did not know the Iñupiaq words for ice. More nuanced for talking about sea ice than English, most people used Iñupiaq when they spoke of ice movement. And ice movement was the thing that worried us most.

"Listen if you hear the camps say, 'Signing off,'" we had been told. That meant the hunters were pulling back from the ice edge, heading to town, and regardless of whether we understood what went before, we should be aware of that. It might mean the ice was becoming dangerous.

"Watch if you see the pack ice start to move."

If it came toward us, narrowing the lead, it was all right as long as the current was parallel to the shore-fast ice. But if the current turned, and the pack moved directly into the shore-fast ice, the resulting collision could send ice blocks miles inland.

"Always gotta watch if you see cracks. Brush the snow away, you'll see what it's doing." Even shore-fast ice could break off and drift away.

Another whaler told us, "Never fall in love with a place. Fall in love with a process." The ice is ever-changing. Love it, but don't expect it to remain the same from day to day.

Some of their advice was hard to follow. The ice was lined with pressure cracks, and we had a hard time telling those that were active breaks from those that were merely surface disturbances. But we tried. We sat where there was a small crack at the foot of the pressure ridge, from the tide lifting it and setting it back. Each time we climbed, we stopped to gently brush away the snow and watch the crack for changes.

We tried to learn the words. *Sikuliaq*, for new-forming ice on the water surface. *Iiguaq*, the less-stable attached ice that accretes along the lead edge. Useful words. But we were scared, most of the time. Scared of the sea ice, and the bears, and of getting lost in sudden fog. I was scared Vera would freeze in her St. Petersburg jeans, and she was scared of the snowmachines because they were loud and fast. We did the best we could, but we were strangers to the ice.

That night after the older whaler left the lead began to close suddenly, the pack ice traveling on an unseen current. The whalers left their tent up but left the shore. We watched the pack ice move closer, frighteningly swift, but passing the lead edge smoothly, in deathly silence. Pieces of the pack churned up and folded under. There were no more birds. Then the sea fog rolled in, blotting out the world.

"Horrible. Is horrible," Vera said, smoking instead of eating, dressed in the thin, tight clothes she would not trade for warmer gear. We were always, always cold, but she had it worse than I did.

"I wonder if we should leave," I said, looking at the rubble of ice and the raw sea fog. But we kept waiting as the pack passed in silence without impacting the edge of the shore-fast ice. When the hour hand touched midnight, the end of our shift, we almost ran to start our snowmachines and ride back to the safety of the bunkhouse, a cold trip back, from flag to flag across windswept new ice.

The fog stayed for days after that, and the wind sprang up from the east again. No birds could travel, but we kept watching. No one was whaling, because the lead was closed. But one of the whalers came out to warn us we should leave the ice until the wind dropped. It was high enough and the barometer dropping so fast that the change in atmospheric pressure coupled with wind could push the water level up, and in turn that sea level rise could cause the ice to break off.

He shouted those things up to us, where we watched on the perch, and we were grateful. I think he thought we should have known already, but he never said so.

It was three days before the weather cleared. We went back out, not sure what we would find. But the perch was still there. The lead was there. And the birds were flying.

Eider eddied over the ice. Guillemots, still white in winter plumage, beginning now to darken into breeding colors. Long-tailed ducks, named *ahalik* for the sound of their voices, and *nigliq*, white-fronted geese. Loons. Jaeger. The sky was so warm and blue it felt like spring at last.

Not long afterward, one of the crews caught a whale. It happened west of the Barrow Spit, but they towed it to the firm ice near our camp. By the time we got there, they'd already moored it in place. We walked carefully to the edge and looked down at the black shape of the whale half underwater, its flippers tied together, touching as if praying. There was such a feeling of joy in the air. People hugged each other, shouting with happiness, "Hey-hey-hey," as they rigged the tackle to pull in the whale. For me also, happy and sad ran together in a blended river.

Early that afternoon, the eider began to fly in earnest, in flocks of tens of thousands that blurred the sky. On shift again, we went back to the windbreak to count. And for a while, nothing else could be thought of. We were caught in a river of birds, almost hysterical, sweating, wanting it to stop, and yet awestruck. And then they were gone, as quickly as they'd come.

That night, after the birds stopped flying, we walked back to the whale again. By then the butchering had begun. Fatigue had set in. But the people were happy. A whale had given itself one more time. We stayed a while with them and were glad, too, for what it meant to the community, seeing the red meat piled on sleds, enough to share, and the weary, fulfilled faces of the elders. In a world changing too fast, where too much had been taken from the community, there was still this, the enactment of a necessary, living bond between the people and whale that stretched back for thousands of years. As if they said, this is who we were. This is who we are.

It took two days for the crews to butcher the whale. In that time, polar bears began to gather. When the hunters were finished, and the last sled load of meat and muktuk had bounced its way toward Utqiaġvik over the overused trail, the bears came in to investigate the carcass. Nothing was left but reddened bones, darkening in the spring sunshine. The bears met to tear at the little flesh that remained. An older male. A mother with nursing cubs. A young male and female that we saw copulate on the blood patch left by the carcass. We watched them as they fed together, established dominance. The mother remained wary, staying apart from the crowd each time she and her cubs began to feed. The others fought or tolerated each other, working over the bones.

Mostly, they were solitary creatures. They fed for a time, then went off to sleep among the pressure ridges. I saw an adult bear eating something white and furry, stained with red, near the whale. One of the cubs, I realized later. In all, we saw thirteen bears at the same time. There may have been more.

After the whale, we counted many birds but never again in the numbers of that astonishing day. The ice grew so weak and the bears so curious, we had to abandon the perch and move on land not long afterward. After that, we watched from the tundra.

On shore, the birds were building nests. Ponds overflowed with meltwater, and snow shrank back from the tundra. Tide cracks formed at the edge of the sea ice. Jaeger and loons passed, shorebirds, and many species of ducks. The fragile, severe beauty of the sea ice and the fear seemed so far away. It stayed in our memories like a dream. A dream until winter came again. And though we were sad, it was also a relief.

Nanuq, Utqiaġvik

◆

Spring 2016

I checked right and left for polar bears as I stepped out the door of the Beijing Hotel. A far cry from China, it was an old plywood ice-fishing shack, still on skids, kept by the Utqiaġvik, Alaska, Wildlife Department as transient housing. Years before, a visiting scientist had painted Chinese characters on the wall, giving it its name. Now I jumped the snow berm at the foot of the steps and trudged in to work.

I had a job measuring whales harvested by Iñupiat hunters. I'd come to Barrow first that spring, when the men were hunting from the ice, and returned in the fall to join the whale scientists. The crews hunted from skin boats west of the Barrow Spit in spring, and in fall from motorboats farther offshore. Each year they were allowed to take around twenty-five bowhead whales. But wind had slowed the harvest that year. We were all waiting. In the interim, I'd been working as a lab tech for the Wildlife Department.

Gabriele was already drinking coffee at the bunkhouse table. Tiny, determined, with blonde curls and a solid little chin, she was my lead that season.

"My little tech," she said, "today we have a special project."

In the back room of the Arctic Research Facility, on a table used for snowmachine repair, she clenched the skull of a juvenile polar bear in a vise. Earlier that year, she said, the cub's mother had been hanging around the village of Kaktovik. Locals hazed her away on ATVs. Somehow then, the cub fell over a gravel bank. That might have caused the injury, though at the time it got up and ran on.

Two days later, the mother swam back, towing the cub. At first, they couldn't tell if it was dead. It wasn't moving, but she stayed with it another day. After that, though, it must have died because she disappeared. Other bears fed on the cub's body before it was brought into the village.

Kaktovik sent the carcass to Gabriele in Utqiaġvik to determine the cause of death. The wildlife veterinarian for the North Slope Borough, Gabriele spent much of her time necropsying animals brought in by concerned hunters and seeking to understand the health of wild populations.

The first work I'd ever done with her was to help necropsy a ringed seal with a cyst at the base of its left flipper. It had been left for us in a body bag on the floor of a lab at the Barrow Arctic Research Consortium. She palpitated the cyst, a fluid bag, under the hide. We rolled the body onto a tarp, and she made a long, shallow cut down the center of its chest and abdomen. When she peeled the hide back, the cyst bulged out, gallons of liquid encased in a weak membrane.

"The question is, is it still infected, or is it an old injury that has sealed over, encapsulating the liquid," she said.

She sliced into it with an ulu, an Iñupiaq woman's knife. A cloudy, pinkish liquid rushed out over her knuckles to pool in the blue tarp on the concrete floor.

"So this was still infected," she said, smelling the fluid and looking at its color.

She held up the edges of the cyst to manipulate the last of the liquid out. I tried to catch it in a Tupperware.

"We'll mop," she said. "Never mind."

"This was a very sick animal," she added. "It's a good thing they didn't eat it. But the hunters know what they are doing. They've been living here for a long, long time."

The last of the fluid out, she turned her attention back to the rest of the animal, splayed open at her feet. "Let's see if we can get this on the table now."

Together, we boosted it clumsily to the steel lab table. The table drain was not hooked up, which was why we did the preliminary cutting on the floor. I laid out Falcon tubes and labeled Whirl-Pak bags as she worked her way through the abdominal cavity, taking samples of major organs, glands, lesions, feces, and stomach contents.

"Histo. Freeze. Histo," she repeated, passing chunks of tissue to me. Kidney. Heart. Liver. Lung. Some would be used for toxicology and parasite studies. Others would end up in the vast midden of the sample freezers, perhaps for decades. Earlier that fall, we'd tried to organize the freezers, grouping samples by species, throwing out unlabeled tubes of nameless tissue or dried-out fecal smears. I'd spent one memorable week defrosting, scraping, and subsampling chunks of walrus colon. Naked, pink, muscular, and unbelievably tough, they carried a smell that lingered on my hands despite double-layered lab gloves.

Now, Gabriele bent over the skull of the polar bear cub. It had been flayed and wrapped in garbage bags before it was sent to her. A bite mark in the skull penetrated through the bone.

"That alone could have killed it," Gabriele said. "It could've run into an adult bear that tried to catch it. They will cannibalize young. Or, the bite wound could have been inflicted after death by bears that showed up to feed on the body after the mother left."

The skull was slippery with fat and blood and still cold from the refrigerator. The eyes were filmed over, the teeth bared. I clenched it between my hands to keep it from rotating in the vise, while Gabriele wielded a bone saw, cutting a careful line around the top of the skull. We wore gloves in case of rabies or trichinosis.

The skull lifted off like a bone cap, showing the intricate, spongy domes of the brain. Soft, purplish, tightly folded, and filmed over with the cloudy skin of the meninges and dark in places with clotted blood. Gabriele picked up a tiny pair of tweezers and used them to manipulate the meninges, exposing a small tear where the bite had penetrated into the brain. The flesh below the tear looked inflamed, and the edges seemed swollen.

"Look at that," she said. "There was time for the tissue to become infected. This bear lived for a while after that first bite. Long enough for its mother to chase off whoever attacked it and bring it in to shore."

She set the tweezers down and used steel scissors to gently clip away a shred of the inflamed meninges and drop it into a test tube.

"This will show it wasn't the hazing that killed the bear. You understand? It's important to the hunters to know."

When she had finished examining the top of the brain, we poured formalin into the skull cavity to fix it, and set it aside. She wanted to dissect the deeper structures of the brain, but for now it was too soft. The formalin would toughen and preserve it.

"Coffee time?" she asked.

I helped her wipe away the bone dust and the fine film of blood from the table. We went back to the kitchen to listen to the VHF radio and see how the whalers were doing. In the front room Benny, who worked for the department, sat cleaning guns, drinking tea, listening to the VHF radio and the slow early-morning chatter of the waking village. Two children played on the radio, squealing to annoy people.

Someone older got on, "Hey, you kids, get off the radio. This is a holy channel."

"Nobody caught one yet," Benny said.

He had the nicest smile. I made two cups of coffee and Gabriele and I sat down too. In the Arctic, on the ice, you have to be patient. Gabriele talked as we sat, saying no one knew how polar bears would react to changing ice. They were hard to survey, and it was expensive.

"Anyway, I am not a population biologist. Body condition matters more than numbers. The bears we're seeing are mostly in good condition. But it is a big deal if a polar bear is killed accidentally. People don't like that. The hunters don't like it."

That spring I worked for a time on a population study that sought to determine how many polar bears were in the Chukchi population through mark-recapture methods. The biologist built wooden boxes baited with whale blubber. Each box held brushes wired in place to catch strands of hair when the bear reached in for bait.

The idea was that bears would scent the boxes from a distance and come to investigate. If follicles were attached to the hairs they left, they could be used to capture DNA and identify individual bears. If it worked, it would be a less invasive and more effective way to study bears than tranquilizing and collaring them, which in any case was unpopular with the Iñupiat. It seemed disrespectful to the animal on a deep level.

From the start, however, the project ran into difficulties, in part because the bears learned how to run the snare line for the bait, so that we caught the same few animals over and over. They even learned how to avoid the wire and get the bait without leaving hairs.

One morning in April, near the beginning of the survey, we snowmachined out on the sea ice to check the snares. We stopped at the tent of a local whaling crew to ask if we could set up a snare nearby. I did not hear their names, but they were welcoming.

"I don't want to draw bears into your camp," the biologist said.

The man shrugged. Smiled. "Anywhere is fine. We live with the bears."

It was true. If the bears were in trouble, it might not primarily be because of their relationship with the whalers. Iñupiat and bears had shared habitat for centuries. Though individuals were killed here, the threat to the survival of the population was at a global level.

We set the snare at a short distance from the trail, baiting it, and wiring brushes to capture hair. Our hands grew numb with cold as oil from the blubber wet our gloves.

"I hope this works," he said, as we climbed back on our snowmachines.

"Me, too," I said.

But in a world of shrinking sea ice, it was difficult even to locate the snares without impacting others on the ice. Once whaling began in earnest, the biologist had to pull many of his sets to avoid friction with the whalers. Conflicts between bears and whalers also intensified. Several bears were killed that spring.

Days later, we drove snowmachines out to a whale that had just been landed on ice near the Barrow Spit. We followed a well-used trail from town, dragging sleds with the heavy harvest boxes full of gear for sampling. As we drove, we passed two of the hair snares, both now unbaited and waiting for retrieval.

The shore-fast ice north of the spit was some of the most stable left in a year of weak sea ice. Three whales had already been landed there. As we drew nearer, we saw their bones at the edge of the lead, even before we saw the whaler's flag. Nearer in, we saw blood-soaked ice; yellowish, withering blubber; and dry, black-red chunks of meat.

The crew began to haul in the whale not long after we got there. We joined the line of pullers, running over trodden snow dragging on the line in a community of effort.

"*Nanuq!*" someone called.

A bear had come near as we hauled on the whale. We saw her first behind the piled ice of a pressure ridge, perhaps a hundred yards away. A white head, peering at us and staying low. It took a moment to focus and see the black eyes and black nose against the absolute white of ice.

"*Nanuq!*"

People stiffened. The bear disappeared from sight. In a moment, she reappeared. She'd circled closer to an old carcass. Warily, she paced into view. A small bear, perhaps last year's cub, pure white and compactly graceful. She stopped to tear at a piece of meat.

"She's just hungry."

"Let her eat."

But she kept moving closer to the line of people hauling on the whale. She nosed a chunk of meat again, her paw pinning flesh, tearing at it, only a few yards away from us now.

"Hey!" someone shouted.

Three of the men grabbed rifles and walked toward her, between the line of people and the bear. They shot into the snow. At the sound of a second shot, she raised her head, looked at the men, and walked haltingly toward them.

They shot to kill. The bullet struck her low on her side. Blood bloomed red, startling and irreparable. Then there was no other way for this to end. She staggered forward a few more steps. Another shot struck her in the hip. Her hindquarters sank to the ground. For a moment she folded together. Her head lifted back up, rearing, still watching the men. The whole time, she had just been watching. We on the line stood quite still, watching back. I think it was a shock to all of us to see it end this way. There were so many moments when it could have gone differently, but they narrowed now to a single inevitability.

The men shot her in the head. She settled to the snow, and lay still, a mound of white fur against white ice. They watched for a long moment to see she if was moving, then walked toward her, shotguns still against their shoulders. Stood over her. One of them toed her with his boot. It was over.

A pale-eyed Iñupiaq man knelt to skin her.

"Shoulda let her scare away."

"She didn't wanna." He was right.

I walked up quietly and touched her hair. She was so soft.

Two days later, at the Barrow Arctic Research Consortium, some of the scientists brought what was left of the carcass of that polar bear in for sampling. I was again labeling Falcon tubes when Gabriele called me to come see. Parting white hair, she showed me the bear's vagina. It was soft and pink like a flower, unhurt.

"Pretty little girl," she said. "Pretty little girl."

But I couldn't look any longer. It was too human.

That night, I left the lab late and walked home. In the last disappearing gleam of light, I saw an Arctic fox playing at the side of the road. A puff of white fur, dancing over the snow, the wind seeming to toss it lightly over the earth. It looked so innocent, but it was not and neither was I.

The People of the Whale

◆

Spring 2017

The whale lay along the ice edge by the time Percival and I reached it. It floated half on its side, its flippers lashed together with heavy line, tied to a stake set in the ice.

"Maybe thirty-footer," a man guessed.

Under the supervision of an elder sitting on a snowmachine, two kids chipped desultorily at the ice on the water's edge, making a ramp for the whale to slide up. The harpooner stepped from shore onto the whale's back. He used a tool like a spade with a sharp blade, to cut a square out of the skin and fat to boil for the crew, *unaalik*.

The women by the tent were boiling water for coffee and food. More snowmachines, guided by the whaler's flag, arrived now from town carrying women in bright parkas and people from other whaling crews, their faces grooved with fatigue.

They greeted each other with "Hey-hey-hey," the whalers' call.

"Hey-hey-hey" spluttered over the VHF from those back in town, a shout of joy, a prayer. Thank you. God bless. The crew's name called over and over.

Now other hunters tramped out a trail, knocking down the ice with axes for the block and tackle to run, to pull in the whale. The work moved slowly. This was the breathing space between the effort of the hunt, the long tow in to shore, and the days and nights it would take to butcher the whale.

Shy, I stood apart, not yet learning people's names. I was a stranger here, afraid of intruding. But Percival nudged me into action. He and I grabbed pickaxes to help. He came from the Utqiaġvik Wildlife Department, scientists sent by the borough to gather data from each landed whale. Two springs before, I'd first come to Utqiaġvik. I returned as I grew to love the place and to respect its people, the difficulty of their lives, the challenges not easy for an outsider to understand, and their glad generosity and grace. Percival was from this place. A thin, imaginative man with a weathered face and bright pink glasses, there was much he understood that I did not. He often tried to protect me and keep me from making mistakes.

At length, the block arrived from town, together with an ice auger. Some of the older men drilled holes into the shore-fast ice and ran a heavy strap between them for an anchor. They ran the block and tackle from the strap around the whale's tail to the anchor point and stretched it out along the trail. Made of wood, the block showed a century of wear, but the line that ran through it was nearly new, only a little faded by the sun. The people would pull on the leading end of the line, running it forward, and falling back to pick up at the beginning again.

"All haaands," a man shouted.

People set their coffee cups down and moved to the line, laughing and calling to each other.

"Walk away . . ."

Grasping the line, we strained at it and felt the whale begin to move. The line lurched forward, as we stumbled over uneven footing. Quickly, we began to sweat, moving faster up the line, falling back, grunting with strain, driven by the calls of the whaling captain, the captain's wife, anyone and everyone working together. The block slid forward, its run shortening, and with it came the whale, slowly beginning to move up on the ice.

"Lock it up!"

The block had reached the farthest part of its run. The crew gripped the lines together, to keep them from slipping backward while they transferred the load from the tow line and reset the block. One of the older men stood with a pickaxe handle through the run of lines, holding it against the block nearest the whale and bracing it so the lines could not twist. It was a dangerous place to be. Blocks could shatter under the enormous tension from the weight of the whale. People had been killed. Some of the blocks had been in use, in this same way, for generations. But the hunters knew what they were doing. The Iñupiat have been a whaling culture for thousands of years, occupying the Utqiaġvik area since probably AD 500. Groups lived along the ice edge here, where the Chukchi and Beaufort Seas meet, hunting whale from skin boats and butchering them in the water.

Yankee whalers first came to the western Arctic in the 1800s, after whale stocks were depleted in eastern waters. Bowhead are a true Arctic whale, never dipping into southern waters, so until then, they had been relatively safe from commercial whaling. When the Yankee whalers arrived, they found tens of thousands of bowhead in the Bering Strait, and later, once the hunt moved north, summering along the coast of the Beaufort Sea. But within sixty years, the population was devastated. Once the whales were depleted, many Iñupiaq starved, despite the resilience of their hunting culture. There were reports of villages along the coast where only bodies were left. Every person was dead of hunger. Others died of smallpox, tuberculosis, diphtheria, or flu, breaking ties of family, tradition, and knowledge.

In Utqiaġvik, though, that history was partly altered by a relationship between local people and a man named Charlie Brower, who arrived in 1886 as a crew member on one of the Yankee ships. Charlie Brower left the ship to live in the village, where he first worked in a trading post and later formed the Cape Smythe Whaling and Trading Co. Brower whaled from shore, borrowing heavily from traditional practices and working with Iñupiaq men and women. They created between them a new and highly effective method of shore-fast ice whaling still in use today. Many of the whalers here were descendants of Charlie Brower and those who hunted with him. Street signs and whaling crew names alike bore their names. Hopson, Brower, Leavitt, Arey. Those families formed a link between cultures at a time when the Arctic was changing fast. They found new ways to survive when whaling faltered, as did the others who shared the trade.

In the years since commercial whaling ceased in 1915 and removed from its pressures, the bowhead population had recovered. Small-scale, shore-fast subsistence whaling, as Brower and the others practiced it, continued under a quota system, feeding the community. Even now, whales are landed in ways used by the Iñupiat people here for thousands of years. It is a link between the hunters and the natural and the spirit worlds. That at least is still true, when so much else has been altered, lost, and found.

Now the block finished its run. Men ran to lock the lines up, to keep them from slipping, while others reset the block, moving the run out farther. The whale's flukes were now on the ice edge, the swell of its body following. The crew stopped to take a break, to drink coffee and pop and cool off. Some of the teenagers and children chipped at the ice again, to smooth landing the whale.

I saw one of the scientists lower her hydrophone into the lead. She squatted at the ice edge, her eyes suddenly happy as she heard the whales.

"They're there!" she said.

In a moment, she offered me the earpieces. "Want to listen?"

I knelt by her, hearing a world of sound: The high, silvery, questioning voices of bearded seals and the unexpected beauty of bowhead songs. The canary-like chirping calls of beluga, somewhere out of sight. And the drumlike beat of the children chipping ice at the water's edge nearby. It was extraordinarily magical. I'd entered a dimension where I could imagine more clearly what these animals sensed.

Bowhead do not echolocate as toothed whales do. Their hearing is adapted to low-frequency sounds that travel far without scattering. They communicate across many miles, with long, musical, low-frequency notes that alter and adapt each season. Unlike many other whales, though their songs are unique to individuals, they also appear to learn and repeat them from each other. No one knows how deeply anthropogenic noise may be affecting bowhead, though they are clearly sensitive to ship sound and will skirt ship traffic by miles if possible. Knowing this, Iñupiat whalers try to ensure there are no ships nearby during the peak migration season.

Songs captured on the hydrophone are clear enough they can be used to pinpoint individual whales over distance. In 1977 the International Whaling Committee briefly closed the Iñupiat subsistence whale hunt due to a low population estimate for bowhead. Whalers rapidly formed the Alaska Eskimo Whaling Commission, and a small hunting quota of twelve whales landed for the nine participating villages was negotiated. Utqiaġvik whalers collaborated with local biologists, using traditional ecological knowledge and a sophisticated array of hydrophones to demonstrate that whales migrate under the ice, rising to breathe in tiny leads or breaking through ice up to three feet thick with their heads. Since this had been thought impossible, their numbers had been severely underestimated by conventional counting methods.

The acoustic data was used to correct the visual estimate generated in the census. After several years of conducting the visual and acoustic hydrophone census, the Department of Wildlife Management scientists presented their revised estimates to the International Whaling Committee, which eventually agreed to the new estimates. Harvest quotas were slowly adjusted upward and revised every few years in response to ice-based censuses and other data. For that spring, the quota stood at sixty-seven bowhead annually distributed among eleven villages. Meanwhile the population has increased rapidly, exceeding seventeen thousand whales by 2011. It may be the most highly regulated hunt on Earth.

Now the crew moved back to the line. Break over. Percival and I joined the others, straining to pull the whale farther in. But it hung up, caught against one of its flippers.

After some discussion, the men rigged a second block hitched to the whip end of the first, multiplying the power of the pullers. By the time we resumed pulling, it was nearly midnight. Already some of the crew looked glassy-eyed with fatigue. Some of them had been up for days, hunting and hauling on the whale, making the most of this brief window in the spring. They were providers, eager to feed their families through the year and to teach, as well, how to live out on the ice as their ancestors did.

It was nearly midnight before the whale came fully up onto the ice. The captain signaled a halt. Kids scrambled up the steep swell of the belly for a picture, their snow boots skidding on wet skin. They perched in a row high above the ground. The crew lined up before the whale.

Trying to stay out of the way, the scientists quickly measured the whale and wrote down a description that might be used to identify it from aerial photographs. People crowded around to hear how long the whale was.

"Twenty-nine feet, nine inches," someone read from the tape, then called the number out to the others.

"Twenty-nine, nine!" someone shouted. Teenagers peered at the data sheet.

"What are you doing?" one of the smallest girls asked.

One of the scientists explained. They were taking samples to keep a record of the whales, for people to study later.

"Are you guys scientists?"

"Yes," she said.

"Is that fun?" one asked.

"Sometimes. Is whaling fun?"

They giggled happily. "Yes. But we get cold!"

Now, the harpooner marked out strips in the blubber using a long-bladed knife on a pole. Each strip was a little more than a foot wide. One of the younger men climbed onto the whale and cut downward into the strip with a spade-like knife. A young girl threw a steel hook attached to a rope up to him, and he thrust it into the leading edge of the strip.

Other women leaned on the rope, peeling the strip back as the man chopped it free with short, quick strokes. It tore loose and fell shuddering to the ice under its own weight. The team of hookers dragged it away at a run, slipping through puddles of melted ice.

The cutter moved on to the next piece. When the strip one meter anterior to the umbilicus came off the whale, the science team followed it to measure its thickness and to take a sample to freeze. It was difficult to slice, stiff with collagen and slippery with oil. The skin itself was over an inch thick, the blubber twelve inches, and on the inner side of the blubber, against the muscle, was a thin layer of hypodermis, a leafy fat. This was the true measure of the fatness of the whale. Whales do not initially metabolize the fat stored in blubber. Instead, they rely first on the hypodermis. A whale's blubber forms a stiff, solid jacket around it, acting as a buoyancy regulator as well as insulation and energy storage. But in time of need, a bowhead can live for as much as a year on its blubber, without eating.

Slipping the piece into a plastic bag, the woman marked it on the data sheet. UV blubber.

"Fat whale," someone said. "It's good."

Two young girls worked their way through the crowd with a steaming bowl. *Unaalik*, the fresh-cooked skin and blubber of the whale. People crowded around them, taking pieces with their fingers, trimming them with pocket knives or eating them straight.

When one of the girls reached Percival and myself, she stopped and offered the bowl. "*Unaalik?*"

I took a bite, happy that they shared with me, conscious I was a stranger there. It was warm and rich, almost sweet to the taste. Fat ran down my fingers. As soon as I had eaten it, I felt a lift of strength and felt a little warmer.

"Coffee?" another girl asked. She was carrying a thermos. A smaller girl followed, her arms full of paper cups. They poured me a cup, viscous with sugar and very hot.

"Thank you," I said, not sure how I could thank them enough. We were all so tired now, I kept forgetting where I was or what I was doing.

Then there was a long pause in the scientific work. We watched as the whale was stripped of blubber. Hours slipped by. They took samples from three different parts of the blubber, at the umbilicus, the flipper, and one meter posterior to the blowhole. The whale shrank as the blubber was stripped off. Blood pooled on the ice.

For a time, I fell asleep on a snowmachine. When I woke, it was very cold. Some of the people had slipped away, but a handful of men were still determinedly butchering. They did not have enough people left to hook the meat. I hesitated, unsure of my welcome, but finally picked up a discarded hook, walked over, and tossed it to the man on the whale. He jammed into the chunk of meat he was cutting without hesitation. I began to pull.

It was exhausting work. The line bit into my hands. But it felt better to work with the others than to watch without joining in. For hours, I kept running and dragging, helping haul the pieces of blubber, each weighing perhaps four hundred pounds, across the blood-slick ice to the piles of shares.

When the blubber was gone, they cut the meat away in huge chunks. These, also, we hooked and dragged to the waiting piles. I helped pack some of it into a radionuclide jar, to be tested later for the contamination that can gather at the poles, particularly in the tissue of long-lived animals. Dense and dark-red, whale meat has a high concentration of myoglobin to allow for oxygen storage during deep dives.

When enough of the blubber and meat had been taken from the carcass of the whale, the abdominal wall was pierced and the contents pulled out on the snow. Some of the older women dragged out the length of the duodenum, the first part of the small intestine, tying it off at one end with a tight piece of string and severing the membrane that held the loops of intestine together with quick, direct cuts from an ulu. When they had a piece that was long enough, they cut it into smaller lengths and stripped the stomach contents from them, squeezing them over and over between their hands. They were still warm, and densely sticky at first, but as they cooled, they became harder to handle with chilled hands.

The skin from the liver was saved too. Most of the organs. The baleen. Near the end, one of the older men from the crew cut the ear bone out to save. It was beautiful, curved and heavy as a shell, immensely dense. Named *siuti*, this bone is traditionally kept by the captain of a whaling crew to remember the whale. No one knows why *siuti* are so heavy, but they are unique to the whale lineage and have been since before whales entered deep ocean waters.

Once the whale had been stripped to its bones, the captain's wife took roll call, calling out the names of crews that had worked on the whale. It would be divided according to tradition, shares in the whale regulated by rules handed down for generations. So much for the captain's feast that the community shared, so much for the boats that helped tow in the whale, so much for the crews that helped butcher, and so on. Some would be shared at the spring feast celebrating the whales, some brought to elders, the rest shared at Thanksgiving and Christmas until nothing was left.

Now the sleds were loaded. People started home across the ice, in the thin light of the Arctic morning. Maybe they would sleep, until the next whale. Percival and I also wearily boarded our snowmachines and drove home in a trance. But our work, too, was far from over; we had another day to prepare for. It was spring, and whaling season had begun.

Spring Whaling

◆

May 2015

"Sure. Yes, I think you should come," John said at last.

He looked at me. We were standing in the back of the ARF, the Arctic Research Facility, in Utqiaġvik, Alaska. He stared at the ceiling with wide, blue eyes as he thought.

"Yes. It will be good for you to see a bad trail. You don't learn much from a good trail."

The whaling season was nearing its end. It was late May, and the sea ice was growing dangerous unseasonably early. South of town the trails were rotting out. The last whale we'd gone to had sunk partly through the ice as it was hauled in. In the end, the captain had had to cut its head off to drop weight, rather than lose the whole whale.

This whale was straight out across the ice from town. There were holes in the sea ice on the trail, we knew. Ordinarily, a stranger like myself would not have gone to a whale like this, but if I did not, John would go alone to collect research samples from the whale.

I dragged my parka on. It was hard to dress for this. It would be hot on the snowmachine but chilly when the sun slid down to a lower angle late at night. John was fixing a throw rope to my snowmachine.

"Just follow me," he said. "When we see black holes. . . . Do you know about black holes in the ice? Those are the ones that go all the way through the ice. No bottom. Well, you'll see. Drive around them. They go straight down."

"We've never lost anyone yet," he added. I watched him, concerned not so much by the whale as by the sheer fatigue on his face. I had great faith in him. Despite his wandering talk, he was always, in the end, one of the men who best understood the world around him, and who looked out first for the people around him.

"You have a shotgun? Good."

I followed him. We crossed the tundra toward town, leaving the ARF, skipping at first the trail that led along the shore. In places the snow was almost gone. Buntings gathered nest material in last year's grass alongside our tracks. We came to a saltwater lagoon where the ice was rotting and gunned our machines across it.

Leaving the land, we picked up a trail that angled out across the sea ice. It was heavily used, a broad swathe of slushy tracks and the skidding marks of sleds. Sun poured down at a low angle, warm and clear out of the blue spring sky, softening the trail. We headed north, out to the lead edge.

Crossing a low-pressure ridge, we came to a pan of younger ice, slick with surface water. John looked back to make sure I was OK. He gestured to me to follow without stopping. I drove exactly in his tracks, seeing the weak ice to either side of the trail.

When we reached the first black hole, he got off his snowmachine and came back to talk.

"See that?" He pointed ahead, to dark water flowing in a small gap in the middle of the trail, the sub-ice current visible. It did look strangely black, such an abrupt tear in the fabric of this world of the brilliant white sea ice. It was chilling to realize how thin the ice really was in places.

We drove around it slowly and kept on. John stopped again before we reached the lead edge.

"The ice out here is pretty unstable, too, Rose," he said. "Just keep an eye on it. We might have to leave in a hurry if things change. Stay close to me."

I nodded. We pulled forward onto the pan of attached ice and parked with our machines facing the trail in case we needed to leave at a run. At the lead edge, the whale lay almost out of the water. She'd been partly butchered, her abdomen opened and the entrails lost in the water. Whalers did that sometimes when the ice was too weak to support the full weight of the whale.

We walked up slowly, quietly. The young boys and men leaning on ice blocks near the whale nodded at us. They seemed glad to see John.

"We had to let her guts go," one man said.

"Oh. Oh yes," John said. "That's right."

But I knew he'd wanted the ovaries. He asked me quietly to walk along the lead edge and see if they had drifted against the ice.

"I should've. . . . My fault. I should've come out sooner. I just had to get some rest." He'd been up all night and into the morning at a different whale.

I nodded and walked along the lead, as far as I safely could before reaching a stretch of trash ice. The sea was soft blue, as pretty as I'd ever seen. But there were no guts left.

Walking back, I found John standing by the whale, talking to one of the older men. They were laughing. John had a way of trying to make everyone feel better.

"Here, Rose," he said. "Look at this."

Where the blubber had been cut away over the lower abdomen, it exposed rich red meat.

"Try it," he said. He cut a bit of the meat and tasted it.

I hesitated, then followed his example. It was very rich.

"It's good," he said. He had a kind of wondering respect in his voice. "Amazing animal. Just amazing. You know, they think bowhead can go a year without feeding?"

"Wow."

I tried a little more.

One of the older men watched me, smiling. "Tastes good," he said too.

"Yes."

John turned away. "We might as well get what we can, Rose," he said.

He asked where the whaling captain was. I knew he was going to ask permission to sample the whale. I walked back to the snowmachines for the data sheets, the blood tubes, and measuring tape. When I got back, we took photographs and wrote the whale's description. The blood was taken from the whale's palate. John knelt at the edge of the ice and stretched out as far as he could over the water to reach the mouth. After a moment's thought, I hung onto his coat. I doubted I could hold him if he slipped, but I could try.

He handed the tubes back to me one by one. When we finished, he wrapped them in a bag and put them in his inner pocket to keep them from freezing.

By then the others were stubbing out cigarettes, standing up from their break, and heading back to the line.

John and I followed the others to the line. He stopped to speak for a moment to an older woman, who stood on an ice ridge by the whaler's flag holding a rifle.

"*Nanuq* was around earlier," she said. Polar bear. She was a pretty woman in a long, flowered parka, her hair graying, and her face worn but beautiful. She looked kind. John talked to her for a moment about family things.

"The nicest woman," he said, after.

We walked away, past teenagers smoking pot at the ice edge. They looked over their shoulders as we passed. Joining the crew, we spaced out along the line. Two men tied snowmachines to the rope, hoping to compensate for the lack of helpers. With a jerk, the whaling captain freed the wrap of line that had braked the block during the rest.

"Walk awayyyy."

The snowmachines roared and skidded on slick ice. We struggled to pull hard, and harder. Painfully slowly, the whale crept forward. Stopped.

"Walk awayyyy."

I pulled so hard I thought my arms would crack. On each side, clinging to the line, the crew was panting, struggling, slipping.

"Walk awayyyy."

But the whale was stuck.

"Gotta let us get more machines on."

"Hold the line. Hold it."

We braced our feet, and kept the line from sliding backward in the block while two teenage boys ran to hook their sleds onto it.

They fastened them with short ties. Kids piled on the back of the machines, to hold them down and give them traction.

"Walk awayyyy."

This time, with four machines, the whale began to move. They pulled and reset, pulled and reset. The whale now was nearly on the ice.

I felt a stir of alarm pass through the crowd. Some of the people stared out to sea, squinting into the low angle beams of the sun. It took me a moment to realize that the pack ice had begun to move. It was coming toward us, toward the fragile shelf of attached ice we stood on, already so much closer than it had been. Every time, it startled me how fast the pack could move.

"Walk away," the captain shouted, trying to recapture our attention.

I grabbed the line. But John came toward me at a fast walk.

"We better get out of here, Rose," he said. I knew he thought that because I was there, but I could not argue. I dropped the line, and followed him quickly toward the waiting snowmachines.

"John. Hey, John," someone shouted. One of the men came after us, waving his arm. "Wait."

John stopped. Took a step. Stopped again.

"It's gonna miss us, look." The man pointed out to sea. "Look. It's gonna pass."

I couldn't see that. I was too much of a stranger to the ice. But I saw John trusted him. I did too.

"All right," John said, after a moment. We walked back to the line.

"If that pack hits, though, Rose," he said. "This ice would crumple. This whole pan would be gone. And these guys can ride faster and cross stuff that you and I couldn't do."

The other man said, "I was there that time they picked everybody up off the ice on the rescue helicopter. Me and my uncles. We tried to run for it, but we were too far. Everybody gotta get picked up that time. But my one uncle and my other buddy, they skipped their machines across the crack and saved them. Brand-new snowmachines."

"The ice broke off?"

"Yeah. First we knew was, they called us. 'You know you guys are moving?' 'No.'"

He laughed as we turned back. It was late evening before the whale was landed. We stayed not to sample but to help, because there were so few helping there. When the whale was landed, we took a piece of blubber. But the guts were already gone. There was no need to keep waiting now.

The sun hung on the horizon at low ebb. We sat down for a while and had a cup of coffee with the women cooking at the tent and the men sharpening knives. Now it was time for the hard work to begin. But we would go home, to wait for another whale, and to remember the people of this crew, this good crew.

On the ride home, the trail had hardened as the air cooled. We rode faster now, wholly exhausted, the sun at our backs but still watching the weak places in the ice. Trusting that the trail would take us home and the ice would hold a little longer. Trusting the whale could be saved, that whales would come again.

Not long afterward, another large whale was caught. It kept breaking through each time they hauled it up. The ice was too soft and weak for whaling now, though it should have been solid a long time yet. The weather had warmed too quickly even for elders to firmly predict a pattern here.

We could only trust that the community would learn anew, in a world in flux, and continue here, living with the ice and snow, the whales and bears. Though in time all things are changed, there would still be people here, and bowhead.

Dinosaurs and Wind on the Colville River

◆

June 2012, July 2017

It was already late evening, though the sun would not set for a long time. So high in the mountains, the air was cold. I watched alone as the light moved silently up the ridge above the river, feeling a kind of awe. I'd been dropped here in the Brooks Range in northern Alaska, to float the Nigu down the Etivluk and the Colville to the sea.

In the morning I launched under a bright, chilly sky, tracing the switchback course of the river. The current slid past ice-covered banks, undercutting them. Midmorning, the wind rose, striking me with the force of a sudden blow, spinning my light boat backward in the river. I pulled off the water and crouched low to let the wind race overhead. It spilled upriver as air heated on the plains below rose into these mountain passes.

Near midnight, when the sun went down, the wind dropped at last. I tried to launch again, to use the pale Arctic night for traveling, but the river lost definition and color in the dusk. I could not see obstacles. At last I camped again, resigning myself to traveling only at dawn. When the sun first rose, I got back on the river until the headwind, rising, slapped me ashore.

That evening it blew so hard the air filled with dust. I pitched the tent, dragged stones inside to weigh it down, and lay spread-eagle on the buffeting floor as the tent bent to the wind. Fine grains of sand sifted through the mesh walls of the tent, filling my lungs and drifting on the floor. I was overwhelmed by it and frightened it would never end.

Steadily, the sand drifted over my body, partly burying me. Sand that was formed from lava perhaps, in spreading centers on the seafloor, ground into dust, reformed into rock, pressed and heated, metamorphosed, and ground away again over millions of years. Rocks that cooled into new forms, rose as mountains scoured by strange winds and gouged by rivers I would never see. Sand that fell away from source rock and slid downriver to some plain and ground into dust over still more millions of years. Sand that now was carried by the wind back upriver, and would itself re-form perhaps one day, giving rise to worlds long after I was gone, and rivers I'd never see.

By dawn the wind had dropped again, and the sand settled. I beat it from my clothes and hair and sought the river. The storm had been almost too much for me.

Three days in, I left the Nigu, entering the Etivluk. The winds grew lighter as the valley widened. Raptors whistled overhead, high, fierce calls, as I drifted below their nests. Caribou hair clotted in the river, and wolf tracks pressed into dried mud. Coming down a series of rapids, I saw a bear burying a kill, circling and tossing dirt. It did not see me, gliding near. The river held me in its current, I could not stop or back away, but I held my breath and traveled safely past.

Leaving the mountains in the lower river, the water broadened and the current slowed. The Etivluk fell into the wide Colville. I passed collapsing banks of permafrost, melting in hot summer sun. Dense, black mud choked the river's edge, swallowing tracks. A band of caribou crossing deep water swam faster when they saw me come around a bend. They scrambled ashore, splashing through the shallows, one miring briefly. Another panicked and turned back in the water, missing its companions' lead. It swam, eyes wide, across the river again to scrabble at a bank too high to climb.

I couldn't stop or move away to ease its fear. The weight of the current forced me on. I saw it try and fail, try and fail to climb the bank. At last, it began to cross the river again, exhausted. I could not see if it survived.

Two weeks in, I still had seen no human traces. Nothing was left since the winter snows. Then, on the riverbank I passed an old excavation half-covered by a worn, blue tarp. Fossils were discovered there in 1961 by a Shell oil geologist. Twenty years later, they were identified as the first dinosaur bones found in Alaska, in a place once thought too cold and dark for dinosaurs. Later, the area was visited again by researchers who found more fragments in the Liscomb Bone Bed, a layer of bone buried in sediment deposited on the Arctic coastal plain around sixty-nine million years ago. They found trackways, too, footsteps where dinosaurs had crossed the plain.

The tunnel I passed was dug by researchers from the University of Alaska. They'd reconstructed the bones of a group of juvenile hadrosaurs that died together, perhaps caught in deep mud. Alaska was warmer then, and the earth had a decreased temperature gradient between the equator and the poles, but even so, these dinosaurs would have seen snow and would have had to live through months of darkness. The researchers speculated they survived by foraging on last year's greens in river bottoms through the winter.

At the time of the Cretaceous extinction, Alaska was a place of humid swamps, cycads and giant ferns populated by small mammals, and marine invertebrates. After the dinosaurs died, the earth began to cool, warming again slightly in the Miocene between 23 and 5 million years ago when kelp forests and grasslands appeared; then cooling slowly in the Pliocene, when humans first diverged from the great apes. Later, between 1.8 million and 11,000 years ago, the earth grew cold, passing through swift cycles of glacial and interglacial periods. Snowfall formed ice caps at the poles. At times, so much seawater was locked in ice that the Bering Land Bridge rose above sea level and animals walked across from Asia, spreading down through the far reaches of the continent. Modern humans arose early in the Pleistocene, during one of those interglacial fluctuations.

Though these climatic fluctuations are apparent through earth's history, what is different in our human era is the rate and source of change and the pace of animal extinctions. Seldom, if ever, in the climatic record has the world altered as swiftly as it has now in response to the chemical emissions of the Industrial Age. So far, the oceans have absorbed much of the anthropocentric warming of our time. But when they reach a point when they can no longer absorb the bulk of the temperature increase, the world as a whole could warm with unimaginable rapidity. We do not know how to survive that. It is outside our experience as a species, as it is outside the experience of almost all living creatures. The world we know has evolved since the last significant warm period.

I thought of a sign I'd seen, held by a child on a street corner in an Alaskan town. "Climate Change is Real. In Other News, Water is Wet." We all knew that; we were living it. But it seemed no one was listening in the government. There was too much money to be made from business as usual.

Now on the Colville, I camped not far from the fossil dig, listening to the silence of Arctic spring. Thinking of the years layered in the banks, exposed now as the river wound its way northward to the plain. Of my own footsteps disappearing as the river took the bank, eroded by melting permafrost. Wondering what would come to this place. Did the last hadrosaur know it was the last one? Did it wonder at some level what had changed?

Years later, I worked for a paleontologist, Hans, near the Bering Glacier on the gulf coast of Alaska, looking for fossil whales in rocks exposed by retreating glaciers. Earlier in his career, Hans had found the remains of whales that walked on land in what is now India and Pakistan, in sedimentary rock that was once the coast of the Tethys Sea, a shallow, warm-water ocean. The Tethys then spanned much of the globe, but it slowly closed as the continental plates rearranged and India collided into Asia, buckling its shores and forcing them up into what is now the Himalayas. The top of Mount Everest is formed of marine limestone made from the shells of creatures that lived beneath that sea before it closed.

Those earliest whales were small mammals related to modern hippos. As they evolved, they lived first onshore, then in shallow coastal lagoons, and finally adapted to spread throughout the oceans of the world. As they began to spend more time in the water, they developed a host of bodily changes. Their nostrils moved farther up their heads, to allow for breathing while partly submerged. Ear bones became isolated from their skulls to allow for directional hearing underwater. The shape of vertebrae changed, allowing for greater flexibility in swimming, while slowly their pelvises lost the ability to support weight. Their hind limbs grew vestigial and eventually disappeared over the course of many million years. Meanwhile, the chemical composition of ancient fossils showed how they had evolved from depending on fresh water to living in salt water, and how at last they lost their need to seek fresh water altogether.

Hans had been the scientist who found the bones that showed much of that progression, working in what were now the hot dry deserts of inland Pakistan. But I met him first in Utqiaġvik, where he'd gone to work with living whales after the war closed the Pakistani borders. One night at the research bunkhouse kitchen table we began to talk about his work with fossils. He said there were few places in the world where near-shore sedimentary marine rocks of that age class were located. One such place had been in the borderlands between India and Pakistan, where he now could not go. The other was the Lost Coast of Alaska, a place of forests, remote mountains, and heavy rain. A place where humans rarely went.

I told him the glaciers were thawing back, exposing rocks that had been buried for millennia. He agreed to fund a trip that summer to travel the coastline and explore the logistics of searching in the area. We left Cordova in early July, flying east as far as Icy Bay, inland over the Bering Glacier. The plane dipped low past outcrops islanded by melting ice. On the way back, the pilot left us overnight on the shores of Lake Roselius, a stretch of water at the glacier face. We made camp there, well above the water in case the glacier calved.

Next day, we worked our way along the shore, looking at rock laid bare by sluffing ice. The fossils we searched for were of whales at the cusp when they first evolved from local populations of near-shore mammals in Pakistan and India to marine deepwater swimmers that populated the globe. Not long after the first whales able to live wholly marine lives developed, odontocetes, the toothed whales, and mysticetes, baleen whales, diverged. Baleen whales stopped developing teeth and evolved instead the keratinous structures they now used to strain water and capture prey. No one knows how that shift occurred or whether perhaps they once had both teeth and baleen. But fifty years ago, a fossil whale skull from roughly that time period was discovered not far from where we were. Though it was eroded and no longer in source rock, the chance existed that others might be found, better preserved, and that they could tell us something of the whales we sought.

I called to Hans when I found fossil shells, ice scarred but still moored in living stone. The carbonized remains of plants and the whorled white marks of ancient shells. Hans came to look.

"That's good," he said, smiling. "Now find a whale."

It was, at least, a beginning. It amazed me just to hold them in my hand, clear white tracing of shells in solid rock that formed so long ago, from sediments laid down at a time when Alaska was slowly accreting from land masses arriving from the southeast. We found a nautilus. Turritella. And once, the teeth of fossil fish. Perhaps there were fossil bones somewhere. Perhaps there were whales.

The following year, we landed first in Taan Fjord, an arm of the sea where the rock was younger than elsewhere on the coast. Earlier that year, a landslip generated a tidal wave when melting ice destabilized the cliffs. Now its shores were scoured raw higher than our heads. At the head of the fjord, the land was stripped bare, a moonscape of fallen rock and melting ice. Its creeks ran red with dissolved minerals. The air was cold, smelling of raw earth; and a great silence hung over us.

Trudging the ruined shore, the mud clung to our boots, exhausting us. I stumbled in one of the rivers, losing my hammer, and was barely able to rise against the blood-red current. Over everything, there lay a sense of awe. A cataclysm too great to comprehend had passed through, and we found few traces of the former world.

When we left that place, we went swiftly, as if escaping something. We traveled on to the Bering Glacier, inland of the Seal River.
Here, too, the land was falling apart as the ice melted. Sinkholes
opened behind us as we walked. Once we saw a bluff face begin to
sluff and realized we stood not on rock but on melting ice. The rivers
ran too deep and wild to cross, their currents high from run-off in
the summer heat. Still we worked our way along their banks, gathering stones from the former world.

Leaving the glacier face, we flew to Kayak Island. Isolated in the
Gulf of Alaska, it was an island like a knife blade made of volcanic
plumes intruding on sedimentary rock. Here Vitus Bering first made
landfall, almost three hundred years ago. His ship was so battered
and his men so weak he stayed only long enough to take fresh water.
But that voyage changed Alaska forever.

We landed there on a stretch of shore below the tide line, late
in the afternoon. We'd never seen the island before, and through a
misunderstanding, the pilot dropped us almost twenty miles from
the lighthouse where we were to stay. By the time we realized what
happened, we had trudged ten miles from our emergency cache at
the landing strip.

With no other choice, we walked all night. The beach narrowed
to a thin line above the tide, choked with debris from winter storms
and tracked by brown bears. Whale bones, ship timbers, fishing gear
lodged in the rocks. There was no moon, and the wind was high.

When at 3 a.m. he grew too tired to walk, I lit a driftwood fire
for protection from whatever animals might be passing. Hans slept a
while; I kept watch with the shotgun balanced on my knees, until the
first gray light began to come. I remember feeling as if I were seeing
visions, but not what those visions were. Only a sense of being in the
presence of some great mystery.

When dawn came fully up, we stumbled on. The sun was high when we reached the lighthouse. It lay at the foot of a volcanic cliff, deserted, buried in wild grass. We went inside, closed the door, and slept for many hours among the rows of dusty bunks, fossils forgotten, glad of human shelter.

But all that was still to come that night on the Colville River. When morning came below the dig, I kept on traveling. I was below the main drive of the caribou migration now. There were only scattered bands, far across the tundra. Here, the riverbanks grew so silty an animal could mire down. And perhaps they would, becoming fossils in a later age.

Years later, where the Chandalar flows into the Yukon, I camped alone one night on an outwash plain. Late evening by the fire, I saw a strange stone beside my foot. A little larger than my fist, stained dark with tannins, it had a pair of lobes with a deep groove between. I set it back and took a photograph. Later, I learned it had been the wrist bone of a woolly mammoth from the Pleistocene.

The river tugged at the bank, collapsing it. The fossil, eroded, could have come from anywhere, tumbled there by the moving water. It was all so impermanent, rocks and water written on a slate washed clean as continents rose and sunk away, and time vanished in the past.

I pulled off the Colville at Nuiqsit, a few miles inland from where it broadened to a delta at the sea. It was summer solstice, the lagoons melting free of ice. The sun never set. Caribou were still running on the hills, and under their feet lay the bones of hadrosaurs.

And all things come to be, and all things pass, and the river keeps running, over the beds of other rivers, long ago, the currents of its passing marked in stone. As our time rises, blossoms, fades, and goes.

Rosemary McGuire works as a biological research technician in the Arctic and Antarctica. She is the author of *Rough Crossing: An Alaskan Fisherwoman's Memoir* and *The Creatures at the Absolute Bottom of the Sea.*